COCA WINE

"A long-overdue, lavishly illustrated historical tribute to Vin Mariani, the coca-infused wine invented by Angelo Mariani in the late 19th century. It was once one of the world's best-known and best-advertised products, endorsed by popes, queens, presidents, actresses, singers, and just about anyone who was anyone. Yes, it contained a small amount of cocaine, but it was only when that drug was isolated as a concentrated white powder that it derived its evil reputation. In the meantime, it inspired (indirectly) Coca-Cola, which unfortunately added a great deal of sugar, though it still contained decocainized coca leaf extract."

MARK PENDERGRAST, AUTHOR OF *FOR GOD, COUNTRY, AND COCA-COLA*

"Historians have long noted the role of Angelo Mariani's pioneering 19th-century beverage, Vin Mariani, in the history of coca and cocaine but yearned for a well-researched biography. This is finally it! Aymon de Lestrange's exhaustive reach and the many beautiful and lavish illustrations—many new discoveries—are alone a treasure. The chapter on Mariani's laboratory and its fascinating products is a rich contribution to knowledge. And *Coca Wine* is so timely: as failing drug prohibitions come into doubt across the globe, we need to know more about the positive cultural roles played by benign coca health products like Vin Mariani, which, like absinthe, may one day soon revive!"

PAUL GOOTENBERG, SUNY DISTINGUISHED PROFESSOR OF HISTORY AT STONY BROOK UNIVERSITY, EDITOR OF *COCAINE: GLOBAL HISTORIES*, AUTHOR OF *ANDEAN COCAINE: THE MAKING OF A GLOBAL DRUG*, AND COEDITOR OF THE *ORIGINS OF COCAINE*

"Aficionados of the divine plant of the Incas in both its natural (coca) and synthetic (cocaine) forms will be fascinated to learn this time-honored (if sometimes reviled) intoxicant was once marketed as a tonic beverage—a fine Bordeaux with a kick—that made the cultured classes across Western Europe and the U.S. acclaim the superiority of Mariani's Coca Wine for both its medicinal and inspirational qualities and unleash a host of competitors, including one enterprising American druggist in Atlanta. Aymon de Lestrange has written the definitive study of this all-but-forgotten recreational beverage, enhanced by exquisite color reproductions of the work of the artists and designers for whom the wine inspired a style that stimulates our senses as much today as it did for our ancestors."

MICHAEL HOROWITZ, COFOUNDER OF THE FITZ HUGH LUDLOW
MEMORIAL LIBRARY AND EDITOR OF THE 1974 EDITION OF
W. G. MORTIMER'S *HISTORY OF COCA: "THE DIVINE PLANT" OF THE INCAS*

COCA WINE

Angelo Mariani's Miraculous Elixir
and the Birth of Modern Advertising

AYMON DE LESTRANGE

Park Street Press
Rochester, Vermont

Park Street Press
One Park Street
Rochester, Vermont 05767
www.ParkStPress.com

Park Street Press is a division of Inner Traditions International

Library of Congress Cataloging-in-Publication Data
Names: Lestrange, Aymon de, 1952– author.
Title: Coca wine : Angelo Mariani's miraculous elixir and the birth of modern advertising / Aymon de Lestrange.
Description: Rochester, Vermont : Park Street Press, [2018]
Identifiers: LCCN 2018011373 | ISBN 9781620557846 (paperback) | ISBN 978-1-62055-785-3 (ebook)
Subjects: LCSH: Coca—Health aspects. | BISAC: DESIGN / Graphic Arts / Advertising. |
    SOCIAL SCIENCE / Popular Culture.
Classification: LCC RS165.C5 L47 2018 | DDC 615.3/23214—dc23
LC record available at https://lccn.loc.gov/2018011373

Printed and bound in India by Replika Press Pvt. Ltd.

10 9 8 7 6 5 4 3 2 1

Text design and layout by Virginia Scott Bowman
This book was typeset in Garamond Premier Pro and Avenir with Starship, Kabel, and Benguiat used as display typefaces

To send correspondence to the author of this book, mail a first-class letter to the author c/o Inner Traditions • Bear & Company, One Park Street, Rochester, VT 05767, and we will forward the communication.

To Marina, Julio, and my children

Illustration by Emil Causé (1867–?) *Supplèment illustré*.
Courtesy of E. Mariani.

Contents

Acknowledgments

. . . .

I would like to thank a number of people who contributed—each in his or her own way—to the writing of this book. First, my excellent and fondly remembered late friend Julio Santo Domingo, who was also very interested in Angelo Mariani and who generously opened his collection of posters and pre-Columbian artifacts to me and, above all, allowed me the unique opportunity to taste Vin Mariani from his rare bottles with their contents intact.

I also wish to thank Arlene Shaner at the New York Academy of Medicine library and Heather Snyder at the Lloyd Library of Cincinnati, for their dedication and competence in providing me all the documents—even the rarest—that I needed for my research.

I also want to thank the Swann Gallery in New York for kindly providing me some photographs of posters from the Santo Domingo collection.

Many thanks also to Chass Vermeulen-Windsant, a great connoisseur of Mariani, who informed me about the several articles on Mariani published in the *Simple Revue,* as well as to Jyri Soininen and Harold Hans Bosman, authors of two excellent recent theses on the history and trade of coca and cocaine, for their guidance in some of my research in this area.

Finally, I would like to mention Mrs. Eleonore Mariani, widow of the grandson of Angelo Mariani, the last owner of the Mariani laboratory, who allowed me to photograph objects and documents that belonged to the great man.

Illustration by Emil Causé (1867–?) *Supplèment illustré.*
Courtesy of E. Mariani.

Introduction

· · · · · · · · · · · ·

The Vogue Beverage
of la Belle Époque

Several years ago, at an auction, I was struck by the beauty of a color lithograph poster from 1897 by the renowned French artist Jules Chéret. It advertised "Vin Mariani," which was destined to become one of the world's most famous beverages. Written in English on the lower part of the poster were the words: "Popular French Tonic Wine. Fortifies and Refreshes Body & Brain. Restores Health and Vitality."

This tonic wine made with coca from Peru, formulated by a Corsican chemist named Angelo Mariani (1838–1914), had been a dazzling success in la Belle Époque, launched by ingenious advertising practices that enabled this coca wine to garner laudatory testimonials from many of the most famous people of the era, from popes, sovereigns, presidents, and ministers to celebrated writers, artists, painters, sculptors, actors, and singers. I was surprised to learn that Vin Mariani was the forerunner of Coca-Cola, which had not only copied the formula—consisting of the infusion of coca leaves in Bordeaux wine—but also Mariani's innovative advertising methods.

Intrigued, I began researching Angelo Mariani, who had once been famous but was now nearly forgotten. An internet search did turn up around twenty-six thousand hits to his surname and seventy thousand for his product, Vin Mariani, but the information was fragmentary and repetitive from one site to another. I first went to the Bibliothèque Nationale, and then later to the Libraries of Medicine and Pharmacy in France and in the United States, and found that Mariani was the subject of very few studies. I also discovered that Vin Mariani had been the most popular prescribed medicine in the world, and that it could also be enjoyed as an

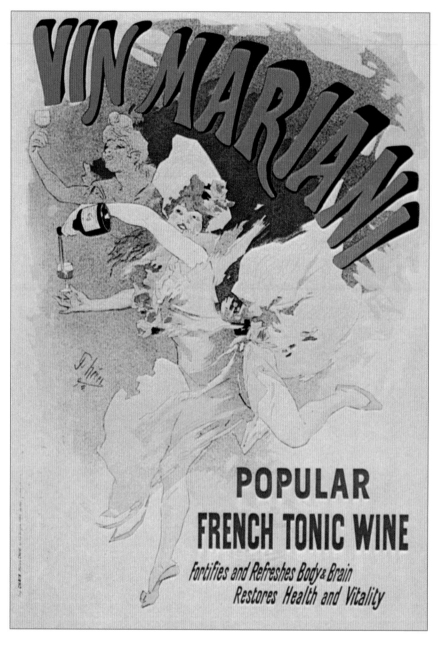

American poster, 1897, of Vin Mariani by Jules Chéret (1836–1932).

aperitif. Its stimulating qualities were especially liked and appreciated by visual, performing, or literary artists, and also by political leaders.

Meanwhile, I started collecting everything I could find about Mariani and his wine. And there was a lot to collect: more than two hundred advertising postcards illustrated by famous artists of that time praising Vin Mariani; silver and bronze advertising medals and objects magnificently engraved to his glory by great medalists; silver jewelry; books written and

Introduction

published by Mariani in France and in the United States on the therapeutic virtues of coca; and lovely illustrated stories singing the praises of Vin Mariani, all of which he himself had funded.

My research and my collection of memorabilia led me to conclude that an illustrated biography of Angelo Mariani was long overdue.

Recent works on the history of cocaine by American scholars, the most serious on the matter, devote at best a few pages to Mariani, but these studies often contain errors, cite very few sources, and focus almost exclusively on cocaine and not on the coca plant itself, a distinction that was important to Mariani.

Since his personal archives and those of his company no longer existed, I had to comb through hundreds of books and articles on coca and cocaine in the Bibliothèque Nationale, in medical and pharmacological libraries in France and the United States, and also in the newspapers of the time to find biographical information on Mariani's life and achievements.

Indeed, I soon realized that Vin Mariani was as much a French product as an American one. Moreover, Mariani himself published more theoretical literature on coca in the United States than in France, due to the extraordinary vogue that he enjoyed in this country; so much so that Vin Mariani was to give birth to the most popular drink in the world today, Coca-Cola.

In the first chapter, after a review of the botany of the coca plant and its history in pre-Columbian times, we will examine its discovery by Europeans through the works of early Spanish chroniclers in the sixteenth and seventeenth centuries. We will note its appearance in literature in 1662 and its study by scientists in the late eighteenth century; samples were sent to Paris in 1749 by the famous botanist Joseph de Jussieu, and naturalist Jean-Baptiste Lamarck gave the plant its name in 1786: *Erythroxylon coca*. In the nineteenth century, it was the doctors' turn to be interested in the plant, from the Italian Paolo Mantegazza up to Sigmund Freud.

Chapter 2 is devoted to Angelo Mariani's early life, including how he came to be interested in coca. We will also explore the unknown history of coca wine in France, its introduction into therapeutics by doctors and pharmacists as well as the even more unknown story of the discovery of the anesthetic properties of cocaine in France in 1880, in which Mariani will indirectly be involved—even though posterity assigns the name of

Portrait of Angelo Mariani by Frédéric Lauth (1865–1922). Courtesy of Les Enfants des Arts.

ANGELO MARIANI
Né à Casevecchie (Corse), le 24 Décembre 1838
Négociant
Membre du Comité de *la Marmite*

Picture of Angelo Mariani in *La Marmite*, 1901.

Introduction

Picture of Angelo Mariani.

famous Austrian ophthalmologist Karl Koller to its discovery in 1884.

In the third chapter we describe in detail the manufacture and content of the product that made Mariani's name famous all over the world: the Vin Mariani à la coca du Pérou (Mariani's Peruvian Coca Wine) and the amazing success enjoyed by this product. We also describe his state-of-the-art laboratory, where he created and manufactured all his other coca-based products: tea, elixir, lozenges, paste, and a concentrated extract.

Chapter 4 discusses the medicinal properties of Vin Mariani and its reception by the medical profession in the United States and in France. We retrace the circumstances by which Mariani and his product became famous in the United States after it was used to prolong the life of President Grant; we also cover the history of the introduction of coca to the United States and France, which is still little studied and known. We will quote testimonials of several American and French doctors of that time who were using Mariani wine in their practice.

Chapter 5 is devoted to the revolutionary advertising methods that Mariani put in place in order to promote his products, methods that in fact made him the father of modern advertising. Notably, he used testimonials by leading personalities of the time who praised the virtues of the wine. These were gathered in fourteen *Albums,* a kind of *Who's Who,* that were illustrated by the era's best artists and that included the biographies of more than a thousand people. Among them we find 3 popes, 16 sovereigns, 8 presidents, 43 ministers, 37 field marshals and generals, 248 writers, 165 painters and sculptors, 30 composers, and 94 opera singers and actors. We will explore the major themes found in the testimonials and drawings in the *Albums* describing the effects of Vin Mariani, namely, eroticism, war, politics, sports, alcoholism, the wine as an elixir of life, and its use as voice tonic. We will describe the enlightened patronage policy that led Mariani to commission authors and famous artists to create delightfully illustrated short tales in praise of coca, and led renowned medalists to create beautiful plaques and medals devoted to coca.

Luxury binding for Angelo Mariani's own copy of the tale *Explication (Explanation)* by Jules Claretie, 1894. The letter "M" in the upper corner designates this copy as Mariani's. Courtesy of E. Mariani. (For more about the coca tales commissioned by Mariani, see pages 101–106.)

Pencil, watercolor, and India ink, 1906, by F. Jacotot (18?–19?).
Courtesy of E. Mariani. The lyrics say:
They are so sweet, Bottle my friend, they are so sweet your small gurgles!
My fate would make more than one jealous, if you were always filled!
Ah! Ah! Bottle, my friend, why are you emptying?

Picture by Nadar of Angelo Mariani with Louis Lumière, Armand Silvestre, and Louis Bourguignon, 1897. Courtesy of E. Mariani.

Chapter 6 looks at Mariani's role as a great host and entertainer. The dinners he hosted at his home on rue Scribe and the annual luncheon at Ledoyen where he invited one hundred guests from all over Paris for the opening of the Exhibition of French Artists were extremely popular. For these occasions, he had amusing menus engraved by the famous artist Albert Robida. Every summer he received many celebrities at his villa in Valescure in the French Riviera.

The first setbacks encountered by Mariani and his flagship product are described in chapter 7. A cohort of imitators in many countries would soon launch their own coca wines, mostly in France, but also in the United States. We will review these imitations, the most famous of which is undoubtedly Coca-Cola. We will tell the story of the creation of this best-selling drink, which, we will demonstrate, was directly inspired Vin Mariani.

Chapter 8 continues the story of the setbacks, legal this time, that were to compromise and put a brake on the prodigious expansion of Vin Mariani. Indeed, the use of cocaine was spreading in the United States (where it had the reputation of being a "Negro's drug") as well as in France, where it will become the fashionable drug of the Roaring Twenties, its popularity aided by pharmaceutical companies that expanded the number of cocaine-based preparations. We will briefly revisit the history of the introduction of cocaine into the United States and France, and cover its reception, which was enthusiastic at first, due to its great therapeutic value, but which became negative with the first cases of cocaine addiction. We will mention its influence on the arts and cinema, on songs and writers. Both American and French authorities quickly recognized the danger of this "national problem." This would lead to anti-cocaine prohibition laws in these two countries, which would have a strong impact on the sales of Vin Mariani. We will also discuss the story of Mariani's company after the death of its founder.

To conclude our survey, we will discuss the issue of coca today. There seems to exist a renewed interest from the scientific community in the therapeutic and nutritional value of the sacred plant of the Incas, and in Andean countries, most particularly Bolivia, a renewed commercial interest seems to exist. Indeed, in 2006 Bolivia elected as president of the republic the former leader of the coca growers' union, Evo Morales, who made coca a central element of his platform by trying to rehabilitate it on the international scene. Commercially, Bolivia and Peru nowadays produce various coca products and, among the coca wines, one is even called Vin Mariani.

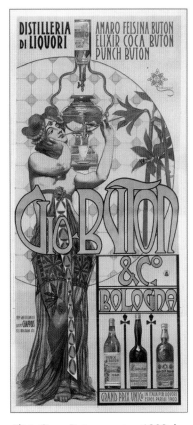

Elixir Coca Buton poster, 1903, by Giovanni Mataloni (1869–1944).

1

A Brief History of Coca

From Pre-Columbian Times to
Spanish Chroniclers to Sigmund Freud

The coca plant's native habitat is on the mountain slopes of the Andean foothills. It is an evergreen shrub that grows a few meters high with reddish-brown bark and small elliptical leaves. It is a member of the order *Geraniales* and the family *Erythroxylacea,* which includes more than two hundred species. Two major species of domesticated coca have existed for ages: *Erythroxylum coca* and *Erythroxylum novogranatense,* with each of them subdivided further into two varieties.[1] Coca was scientifically

Coca harvesting
in Bolivia.

described for the first time in 1749 by the French botanist Joseph de Jussieu (1704–79). The naturalist Jean-Baptiste Lamarck (1744–1829) gave the name *Erythroxylon coca* to the plant in 1786.

Engraving of a coca plant.

Drawing of a coca plant given by Mariani to the Museum of Natural History, Paris.

The oldest archaeological traces of coca chewing were discovered in Peru and Ecuador. In the Nanchoc Valley in Peru, the radiocarbon dating of leaves indicates that coca chewing began at least in 6050 BCE. In Ecuador, excavations unearthed small limestone containers from the Valdivia

A Brief History
of Coca

culture (ca. 2000 BCE).[2] On the sites of Culebras (2500–1800 BCE), Asia I (1800 BCE), and in the Chillon Valley (1900–1750 BCE) and Ancon (1800–1400 BCE) in the south of Peru, archaeologists discovered bags filled with coca leaves as well as limestone containers.

Coca alkaloids were also detected in the hair of mummies from 1000 BCE that were found in northern Chile.[3] Earthenware figures showing the characteristic cheek bulge of the coca chewer have been found in different pre-Columbian cultures, among them the Mochica and Nazca cultures (100 CE).

Figurines of coca chewers from Narino, Colombia, (ca. 400 BCE–600 CE). Courtesy of J. Santo Domingo.

Coca played a very important role in medicine, religion, leisure time, and work for the Indian population. During the Inca dynasty (thirteenth to sixteenth centuries), the coca-chewing habit spread among the population. The Incas controlled major plantation areas and trade routes through their military conquests. Coca became a state monopoly, and its use was regulated by the Incan governor.[4]

A Brief History of Coca

Calero (limestone container) pre-Inca (tenth–twelfth century CE).
Courtesy of J. Santo Domingo.

Figurine of a coca chewer, Jama Coaque, Ecuador
(ca. 400 BCE–400 CE).
Courtesy of J. Santo Domingo.

Amerigo Vespucci (1454–1512), the Florentine navigator who gave his name to the American continents, also gave the world the first account of coca in 1504. In a letter to Pier Soderini, he writes that he found an island where

> They all had their cheeks swollen out with a green herb inside, which they were constantly chewing like beasts, so that they could scarcely utter speech: and each one had [suspended] upon his neck, two dried gourds, one of which was full of that herb which they kept in their mouths, and the other [full] of a white flour, which looked like powdered chalk, and from time to time, with a small stick which they kept moistening in their mouths, they dipped it into the flour and then put it into their mouths in both cheeks, thus mixing with flour the herb which they had in their mouths: and this they did very frequently.[5]

According to other sources it was the Dominican friar Tomás Ortíz (1470–1538) who, in 1499, was the first Westerner to mention coca.

Amerigo Vespucci
(1454–1512).

A Brief History of Coca

With the conquest of Peru by Francisco Pizzaro (1478–1541), several chroniclers and friars provided other accounts in stories of their travels. The historian Gonzalo Fernández de Oviedo (1478–1557) was the first to describe the physical effects of the plant in 1535: "the Indians say that this herb removes thirst and fatigue, [...]* headache and pain in the legs."[6]

According to a letter sent to Emperor Charles V in 1539 by the Dominican bishop of Lima Vicente Valverde (1498–1541), the coca

> Is one thing that the Indians are never without in their mouths, that they say sustains and refreshes them, so that even under the sun they don't feel the heat, and it is worth its weight in gold in these parts and the main income of the tithe.[7]

The conquistador and chronicler Pedro Cieza de León (1518–54), gave a precise description of coca chewing in 1553:

> Throughout Peru the Indians carry this coca in their mouths; from morning until they lie down to sleep they never take it out. When I asked some of these Indians why they carried these leaves in their mouths (which they do not eat, but merely hold between their teeth), they replied that they hardly felt hunger, but were full of strength and energy.[8]

He provided details on the cultivation of coca and the taxes it brought to Spain, and he noted that "there are some persons in Spain who are rich from the produce of this coca, having traded with it, sold and resold it in the Indian markets."

In 1555, the historian Agustin de Zarate (1514–60) noted that:

> In certain valleys, among the mountains, where the heat is very strong, grows a certain herb called coca, which Indians do esteem more than gold and silver [...] the virtue of this herb, found by experience, is that any man having these leaves in his mouth never feels hunger nor thirst.[9]

The shape of coca leaves can be seen on the inner binding of Angelo Mariani's own copy of the tale *Explication* (Explanation) by Jules Claretie, 1894. Courtesy of E. Mariani.

---

*Due to the nature of the quoted material, which often used ellipses in the original source, it should be mentioned that I have used square brackets to show instances where I have inserted ellipses to break the text. Where there are no brackets, the ellipses are original to the quote. Further, credit for quote translations can be found in the notes section. Where not noted, the translation is my own.

Dessin de A. ROBIDA.

Postcard by Albert Robida (1848–1926).

The attitude of the first Spanish conquerors and of the Catholic Church toward coca was ambivalent. The debate would rage throughout the sixteenth and early seventeenth centuries between prohibitionists and antiprohibitionists. Part of the clergy and some chroniclers favored the ban because they considered the plant a remnant of paganism, since it was used in pagan religious ceremonies and was thus an obstacle to the conversion of the Indians. In particular, they thought that it prevented the Indians from eating properly, since land was cultivated for coca instead of food crops, and so coca prevented them from properly taking care of themselves because malnutrition made them more vulnerable to diseases.

The antiprohibitionists, however, believed in the healing properties of coca and saw it as a key stimulant for the Indians and as a dietary supplement. They also thought that, since the Indians were Christians, prohibiting coca might make them become pagans again. They argued further that their work in silver mines would be compromised if coca was banned. The lawyer and economist Juan de Matienzo (1520–79), one of the strongest antiprohibitionists, felt that the plant, a gift of God, was essential to maintain the presence of Spaniards and that removing coca would "mean that [there] would be no more Peru."[10]

The prohibitionists tried to forbid its use in 1552 and again in 1569 at the first two Ecclesiastical Councils in Lima. Their failure was partly because of the opposition of the bishop of Cuzco, who believed in the virtues of the plant and in the revenues that it produced. Finally, the arguments of both camps were presented to Philip II, king of Spain. In 1569, in an edict, the king made a concession to prohibitionists, stating that the Indian beliefs that held that chewing coca gives strength "is an illusion of the devil." But at the same time, he rejected the idea of prohibition, seeing coca as something that mitigated the severity of their working conditions.

The Spanish colonial government had actually realized that allowing coca chewing was essential to recruiting Indians for arduous labor such as work in the mines. This became especially true with the discovery of the silver mines of Potosi in 1545. The working conditions were particularly difficult at that 13,000-foot altitude. The Spanish figured out that promoting coca consumption among the miners led to an increase in silver production.

They soon realized the profit that they could also make from this miraculous crop and they managed to achieve a monopoly of its sale. In 1567, an estimated 2,000 Spaniards (8 percent of the European population in the viceroyalty of Peru), were involved in the coca trade. At the same time, an estimated 300,000 adult Indians consumed coca, nearly 20 percent of the population.[11]

The physician and botanist Nicolas Monardes (1493–1588) was the first to describe the psychoactive properties of coca leaves in 1574:

Nicolas Monardes
(1493–1588).

> When they will make themselves drunk and be out of judgement, they mingle with the Coca the leaves of tobacco, and chew them all together, and go as though they were out of their witts, or if they were drunk, which is a thing that doth give them great contentment to be in that sorte."[12]

His book on the medicinal plants of the New World was translated into six European languages and went through forty-two editions in the one hundred years that followed.

In 1590 the Jesuit José de Acosta (1540–1600) devoted a whole chapter of one of his books to coca with details on the plant's botany, its use, and the annual consumption of coca leaves, and notes that:

> In the time of the Incas it was not lawful for any of the common people to use this coca without license from the Governor. [. . .] Many grave men hold this as a superstition and a mere imagination. For

Coca Appearing to the Conquistadors. Engraving by Albert Robida (1848–1926).

my part, and to speak the truth, I persuade not myself that it is an imagination, so as to go some days without meat, but only a handful of Coca [. . .]. The Lords Yncas used coca as a delicate and royall thing, which they offered most in their sacrifice, burning it in honor of their idols."[13]

In 1605, the first detailed mention of coca in a French text was published by the magistrate Claude Duret (1570–1611) in his botany book.[14]

In the following years, the medical properties of coca were described by two Jesuit chroniclers, Blas Valera (1545–97) and Bernabé Cobo (1582–1657).

In his lost works on the history of the Incas, from which Garcilaso de La Vega published some extracts in 1617, Blas Valera wrote:

> Coca preserves the body extraordinarily from many infirmities and our doctors use it powdered for application to sores and broken bones, to remove cold from the body or prevent it from entering, as well as to cure sores that are full of maggots. It is so beneficial and has such singular virtues in the cure of outward sores, it will surely have even more virtue and efficacy in the entrails of those who eat it. [...] The greater part of the revenue of the bishops and canons of the cathedrals of Cuzco is derived from the tithes of the Coca leaves.[15]

Mariani would design a product that's many benefits included relief from pain, as can be seen in this watercolor painting of a drunkard by Charles Pezeu–Carlopez (18?–19?)

The anesthetic properties of coca leaves were first discovered by the Jesuit Bernabé Cobo who, in 1653, mentioned that toothaches could be alleviated by chewing coca leaves:

> This happened to me once, that I called a barber to have a tooth pulled, that had worked loose and ached, and he told me that it would be a pity to pull it because it was sound and healthy; and a monk friend of mine who happened to be there, advised me to chew coca for a few days. I did so, soon to find my toothache gone.[16]

A few years later, in 1662, the first mention of coca in English literature occurs in a long poem titled "The Legend of Coca," written by Abraham Cowley (1618–67):

> *Mov'd with his Country's coming Fate (whose Soil*
> *must for her Treasurers be exposed to spoil)*
> *Our Viracocha first this Coca sent,*
> *Endow'd with leaves of wond'rous Nourishment,*
> *Whose juice Suck'd in, and the stomach Ta'n*
> *Long Hunger and long Labour can sustain [...]*
> *Nor coca only useful art at Home,*
> *A famous Merchandize thou art become; ...*[17]

Abraham Cowley (1618–67)
by Sir Peter Lely.

The Dutch botanist and physician Herman Boerhaave (1668–1738) was the first to mention coca in a "Materia medica" published in 1708. He observed that the bitter principles of the juices of the coca leaves yielded a "vital strength" and provided "genuine nourishment."[18]

But, strangely enough, coca was not mentioned in later editions of his book or in his later writings. Perhaps this was due to the difficulty of getting adequate supplies of fresh coca leaves.

It is only in the decades that followed that scientists had the opportunity to study coca directly from samples. In 1735, an expedition to the New World was sponsored by the French Academy in order to measure an arc of the meridian at the equator, to verify the shape of the earth. The

A Brief History
of Coca

expedition was headed by the mathematician Charles de La Condamine (1701–79) and counted among its members the botanist Joseph de Jussieu (1704–79).

Jussieu spent thirty-six years in Peru, Bolivia, and Ecuador collecting botanical samples. Unfortunately the coca samples that he collected never reached France. He returned to France in 1771 in a state of physical and mental decline, having left behind crates of manuscripts and botanical samples that, unfortunately, were never found.

In 1749 he managed to send a few samples to his brother Antoine de Jussieu (1686–1758) at the Museum of Natural History in Paris, where they were examined by the famous Swedish botanist Carl von Linné (1707–78) and then by the French botanist Jean-Baptiste de Lamarck (1744–1829).

Carl von Linné (1707–78).

The latter placed the plant in the *Erythroxylaceae* family under the name of *Erythroxylon coca* in 1786.[19]

The following year the Jesuit Antonio Julián (1722–90) in his book on the New World lamented that coca was not used in Europe alongside tea and coffee:

> It is a pity to reflect that so many poor families cannot obtain this preservative against hunger and thirst; that so many employees and workmen lack this help for sustaining their strength in their long, continuous labors; that so many old and young people who apply themselves to the task of study, of composition, and of literary work, cannot enjoy the benefits of this plant against the exhaustion of vital power, the debility of the brain, and feebleness of the stomach, which are inseparable companions of ceaseless mental effort.[20]

In the middle of the nineteenth century travelers and then scientists became more aware of the astonishing therapeutic virtues of the plant.

Among them was the famous Italian neurologist, physiologist, and anthropologist, Paolo Mantegazza (1831–1910). He worked as a doctor in Salta, Argentina, during the years 1854–58. The visits that he made to the northwest of the country made him acquainted with the Indian habit of chewing coca. He started to experiment with it regularly on himself, gradually increasing the doses. In a seventy-page article on the medicinal virtues of the coca published in 1859, he reported that he once chewed sixty grams of coca leaves in one day. He noted that "it was the only time

Jean-Baptiste de Lamarck (1744–1829).

A Brief History of Coca

that I fully experienced the delirium of the inebriating effects of coca at its ultimate limits, and I must confess that I found this pleasure superior to all the other physical ones known to me so far." He described this experiment and the wonderful visions he obtained in these astonishing terms:

> I sneered at the poor mortals condemned to live in this valley of tears while I, carried on the wings of two leaves of coca, went flying through the spaces of 77,438 worlds, each more splendid than the one before. An hour later, I was sufficiently calm to write these words in a steady hand: God is unjust because he made man incapable of sustaining the effect of coca all life long. I would rather have a life span of ten years with coca than one of 1000000.... (and here I have inserted a line of zeros) centuries without coca.[21]

Paolo Mantegazza (1831–1910).

Postcard by Paul Avril
(1849–1928).

Composition de Paul AVRIL,
Artiste peintre,
pour *l'Album Mariani*.

A Brief History
of Coca

Mantegazza recommended its use to cure, among other things, coffee addiction, toothache, stomach disease, and nervous and mental sickness, and he also recommended it as an aphrodisiac.

Mantegazza's text became widely read among the scientific community. One of its readers was Sigmund Freud, who in 1884 wrote in his famous article "Über Coca" ("On Coca"):

> Mantegazza is an enthusiastic eulogist of coca and illustrated the versatility of its therapeutic uses in reports of case histories. [...] However, I have come across so many correct observations in Mantegazza's publication that I am inclined to accept his allegations even when I have not personally had an opportunity to confirm them."[22]

At the time of Mantegazza's experiments, Archduke Ferdinand of Austria sent the frigate *Novara* on a circumnavigation that would last from 1857 to 1859. Before its departure, Dr. Friedrich Wöhler (1800–82) of Göttingen requested that the naturalists on the expedition bring back a large quantity of coca leaves so that he could carry out a thorough investigation of coca and extract its active principle.

In September 1859, Dr. Wöhler received thirty pounds of the precious merchandise and gave it to his student Albert Niemann (1834–61) to analyze. He soon discovered an unusual crystalline organic base that he called "cocaine."

He published the result of his research in a doctoral thesis in March 1860.[23] He died the following year, ignorant of the great impact that his thesis would have on the scientific community and of the fortune of this new molecule. But that is another story.[24]

Mantegazza's text also had another famous reader: the French pharmacist Angelo Mariani.

Mariani's product can be seen in the background of this illustration by Louis Morin (1855–1938) from the coca tale *Trois filles et trois garçons* (Three Girls and Three Boys), 1899.

2 Angelo Mariani, Father of Coca Wine

. . . .

The Beginnings of Vin Mariani,
Which Would Become the Most Popular
Prescribed Medicine in the World

On April 6, 1914, a huge crowd thronged the church of La Madeleine in Paris to attend the funeral of Angelo Mariani, who had died on April 1 at his home in Valescure on the Riviera. In the crowd were, among others, the former president Paul Doumer; General Gallieni; the Duke of Choiseul-Praslin; the great opera singer Hortense Schneider; and the writer Jean Richepin. After the service, friends and staff of Mariani's company went to Père Lachaise cemetery, where they were joined by a crowd of reporters and onlookers.

In front of the tomb, the painter Théophile Poilpot (1848–1915), a close friend of the deceased, said:

> No biography need be written of Angelo Mariani, as he is known worldwide for his kindnesses and for his philanthropy, the effects of which will extend to infinity. No suffering or sorrow left indifferent this great heart, whose whole existence was devoted to softening the misfortunes of others. He has long given away all the proceeds of his work without thought of himself, happy, joyful to do so, and with the most touching simplicity; because, ladies and gentlemen, Angelo Mariani is the rarest example of those who know how to give.[1]

ELIXIR PERUVIEN

Poster project, 1902,
by Leonetto Cappiello
(1875–1942).

Séverine (1855–1929), the libertarian journalist and feminist, wrote
in *Le Gil Blas:*

There was nothing of the charlatan in this launcher of a unique business, who was the first to believe in it, and for an advertisement was
happy with the portrait and autograph of his friends. Nor was he a

Angelo Mariani,
Father of Coca Wine

patron who was changed by money. No presumption or bragging—no swollen ego. Toward the things of the mind, he felt, he professed, a kind of timid reverence. He worshipped beauty, and had respect for art and artists. He did not protect them (as protection involves an element of humiliation), but helped them fraternally [...] because it was his goodness that was the secret of his prestige, of his real influence. It is by goodness that he reigned, and he will remain immortal in the hearts of those who knew him.[2]

Rachilde (1860–1953), a famous novelist of the time, wrote in *La Vie* that Mariani had invented

The elixir of the imagination, the spirit of his delectable wine, was such for many spiritual people. He knew how to pour out his nectar on crowned heads as well as on lesser poets still in need of a principality! [...] This excellent man not only gave his wine to all the men of letters but also his flowers to all the women. [...] He is dead, and all men of letters, all the poor overworked brains, should mourn his memory, because he was the benefactor of those who are the most difficult to please, people of taste.[3]

His obituary in *Le Figaro* pointed out that Mariani had known the great politicians Gambetta and Thiers, as well as Alexandre Dumas, fils, Charles Gounod, Sarah Bernhardt, and Victor Hugo.

The obituary referred mainly to his life's work: the coca wine that bore his name and made him famous around the world and also noted that he was "one of the most popular men of his time: he knew everybody and everybody loved him."[4]

His death coincided with the end of an era commonly called "la Belle Époque," a twenty-year period in which France enjoyed unparalleled prosperity and during which Angelo Mariani and his wine achieved an unrivaled success.

Angelo Mariani was born Ange-François Mariani on December 17, 1838, in Pero Casevecchie, Corsica, son of François Xavier Mariani (December 29, 1810–December 2, 1875) and Sophie Sebastiani (August 21, 1821–March 6, 1904). He was the eldest of seven children.

Sophie Mariani (1821–1904), mother of Angelo Mariani, by Jules Lefebvre (1834–1912). Courtesy of E. Mariani.

Angelo Mariani, Father of Coca Wine

Mariani's father was a pharmacist in Pero Casevecchie and then after 1847 in Bastia. Very little is known about Angelo's youth or about his studies except that he was, for a while, an assistant at his father's pharmacy in Bastia. And little is known about the precise date of his arrival in Paris, which was probably between 1860 and 1863. A book on the history of Corsica published in 1863 mentions a "young Angelo Mariani" among the names of Corsicans living in Paris at this time.[5] We know that he started as an apprentice, first in the Chantrel pharmacy located on rue de Clichy, and then in Mondet at 108, rue de Grenelle, where he was responsible for the development of new tonics to cure anemia. He first worked on cinchona bark extracts, preparing and selling various preparations under the name of Quinquina Mariani. He published a small monograph on cinchona's medicinal properties.[6]

Advertising placard for Quinquina Mariani, 1870. Courtesy of E. Mariani.

Angelo Mariani, Father of Coca Wine

Focusing as he did on making herbal tonics, it was inevitable that he would come across the coca plant. The plant had begun to be the subject of serious medical study: in the ten years following the article by Mantegazza in 1859, at least three pamphlets, three theses, and six articles on coca would be published in France.

When did Mariani become acquainted with coca and begin to market it? It is difficult to determine the exact date. Mariani himself mentions both 1863 and 1867. Other contemporaries say it was 1865, 1866, or even 1869.[7]

In an important biographical article published after Mariani's death, the novelist and journalist Georges Régnal said that one day "Before or after the 1870 war," Mariani came across a booklet on Peruvian coca, which was "almost unknown in Europe, favorite of the Indians who chewed it to sustain their strength during long walks. Thus was the idea found."[8]

A close friend, Dr. Charles Fauvel (1830–95), a throat specialist and the father of modern laryngology, encouraged Mariani to continue his research. In 1869 he had found that the application of an extract of coca concentrated on the membrane of the larynx had an anesthetic effect. In his 1884 article on coca Sigmund Freud quoted Dr. Fauvel, for whom coca was the "best tensor of the vocal cords." According to Mariani, "he is the one who first had the honor of demonstrating the anesthetic properties of coca." Fauvel described its properties:

> I popularized this plant in France beginning in 1869. . . . Since then, I haven't stopped using aqueous or alcoholic solutions of concentrated coca in local applications on the pharyngolaryngeal mucosa either in my private practice or at my clinic. [. . .] I always get quite pronounced anesthetic effects.[9]

Angelo Mariani made his first experiments mixing coca leaves with alcohol, but without satisfactory results. He then decided to use a red wine from Bordeaux, and Vin Mariani was born. Several articles have described the story of the very first client of the new preparation.

According to Georges Régnal, a female singer came to see Mariani on the advice of Dr. Fauvel. He made her taste

a few drops of his new preparation. [. . .] The diva dipped her lips into the glass containing this small sample, tasted it, meditated a

Doctor Charles Fauvel
(1830–95).

Angelo Mariani,
Father of Coca Wine

while, and after a moment said: it is excellent, you'll send me a dozen bottles. Vin Mariani existed! The client's order brought about the consummation of its now fixed formula.[10]

A medical article provides more details:

Miss B., opera singer, aged twenty-two, consulted Dr. Ch. Fauvel April 16, 1869.... The patient complained of hoarseness dating back about four months, being resistant to all medications used until then. [...] Doctor Fauvel prescribed the coca in the form of Vin Mariani. No other medication. On the seventh day, there was a noticeable improvement in the tone of voice. The patient may, after fifteen days, resume her singing exercises. The general condition is gradually improving. [...] After three months of daily use of Mariani's coca wine, her health was completely restored and her voice had recovered all its purity.[11]

Dr. Charles Gazeau said in another article that the artist was "affected the last eight months by a granular pharyngitis with a hypertrophy of the tonsils." After treatment with Vin Mariani, her voice was "clear and vibrant as in the past, so much so that . . . Miss B., whose career seemed likely to be broken by her illness, is now acclaimed in London, where she has a huge success."[12]

A journalist from *Le Figaro* believed that Miss B. was an actress, not a singer, and implies a different date, earlier than 1869. He wrote of the episode:

Chance pulled him from the shadows. In the back of the shop he was mixing some coca leaves with a kind of liqueur when a very pretty young woman came in and asked the young chemist if he had a cordial to give her. She is an actress, rehearsing a play at the Vaudeville Theater by an acclaimed author who, at the rehearsals, requires considerable work from his players. The acclaimed author's name is Victorien Sardou, and the play is *Maison Neuve*. Mariani brings his liquor. The actress tastes it. She tastes it again. "Send me twelve bottles of it. What is that?" "I do not know. It is a wine that I make for myself." "Well! You will make it for me too. Miss Cellier, from the Vaudeville."[13]

"Between France and America, there is sympathy as natural as the one between wine and coca."
—Paul Claudel, writer; *Supplement illustré*, 1926–27

Angelo Mariani, Father of Coca Wine

In time, others developed their own coca wines and products, as seen by this decorative box containing a bottle of coca wine Vin de la Madeleine. Courtesy of J. Santo Domingo.

Angelo Mariani, Father of Coca Wine

We know that the opening of this play by Victorien Sardou took place in December 1866. So it was at that time, according to the journalist, that Mariani made the discovery that made him famous.

But Mariani was not the first to use or market coca wine.

In the first thesis on coca, written in 1862, Louis Gustave Demarle mentioned, without further details, the administration of a "wine prepared with coca on a chlorotic woman."[14] In an article on the "Physiological Action of Coca: Its Therapeutic Use" published in the *Journal des connaissances médicales pratiques* (Journal of Practical Medical Knowledge) dated January 20, 1863, we find one of the earliest references to coca preparations. Its author, Dr. Reis, writes that having received from Lima a small supply of coca leaves: "I asked one of our most educated and distinguished pharmacists, Mr. Fournier, to pulverize for me some coca leaves." He made lozenges, a syrup, and finally, "An elixir primarily intended to be administered after meals as a table liqueur" consisting of 100 grams of coca leaves, 700 grams of alcohol, and 300 grams of sugar. The author gave us the recipe:

> Coarsely crush the leaves, then drain them in a displacement apparatus with 700 grams of alcohol; vigorously express the residue; boil it in 300 grams of water and use this decoction to make, with the 300 grams of sugar, a syrup that you will mix with the tincture previously obtained. Filter after forty-eight hours of contact.[15]

He claimed to have administered it in some cases of chronic diseases, "With the sole purpose of sustaining and reviving strength." In 1866, Dr. Reis published another article, mentioned by Freud in his study of coca, entitled "Note on the Use of Coca in Therapeutics, and Particularly in the Treatment of Cholera."

The same year, in 1863, the Parisian pharmacist Joseph Bain sold preparations with coca that he advertised in brochures that praised its medicinal virtues. It is very likely that he was the first in France (which he himself claimed)—and to our knowledge perhaps in the world—to market a coca wine. He also concocted a coca elixir composed of 100 grams of coca leaves, 300 grams of 80 percent alcohol, and 300 grams of sugar, as well as a "nutritional tonic wine with cinchona and coca," and coca lozenges. He also later produced a coca "spirituous water" that was meant to be used as a toothpaste, and a concentrated coca elixir, four times more

Label for Vin tonique et nutritif Bain au quinquina & coca
(Bain's Nutritional Tonic Wine with Cinchona and Coca).

Printed metal advertisement
for Elixir Péruvien Coca Lacaux
(Lacaux's Peruvian Coca Elixir).

powerful than the ordinary elixir. It should be noted that these preparations were for sale at the pharmacy of the same Fournier who had prepared a coca elixir for Dr. Reis with coca leaves he had provided.[16]

On May 26, 1865, the brothers Jules and Charles Lacaux, liqueur sellers in Limoges, filed a patent for their Peruvian Coca Elixir. In 1873 they created a distillery that would run until 1914, when it was replaced by a paper mill which is still in operation today.

A few years later, in 1867, another Parisian pharmacist, Chevrier, marketed a coca wine, as well as an elixir and coca lozenges.[17]

Mariani may not have been the first to market coca, but he is the one who made its therapeutic properties known worldwide. The creation of his elixir was an amazing breakthrough which contributed, in its own way, to la Belle Époque's frenetic artistic and scientific creativity.

In 1872 and 1875 Mariani published articles on the history and virtues of coca in two medical journals.[18]

Angelo Mariani,
Father of Coca Wine

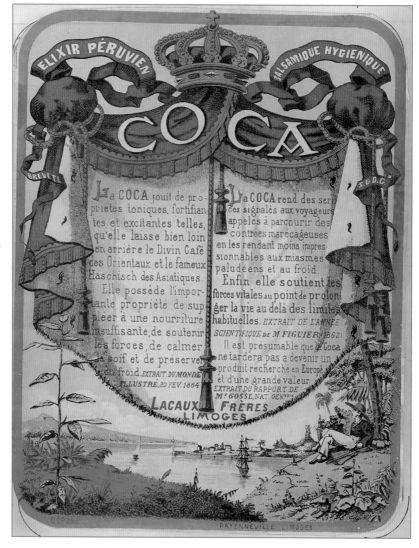

Label for
Lacaux's Peruvian
Coca Elixir.

Excited by the properties of his preparation, Mariani improvised a laboratory in his small apartment at 19 rue Vaneau, where he lived with his wife, Marie.*

---

*His wife, born Marie-Anne Paulmier on March 18, 1846, and whom he married on August 4, 1870, died at the age of thirty-one on January 26, 1878. Mariani remained a widower throughout his life. Marie-Anne gave birth to a boy, André, born on June 2, 1871, who died in April 1878, a daughter, Andrée, born on August 8, 1874, who died at the age of nineteen on April 23, 1894, and a son, Jacques, born on October 4, 1875, who became a pharmacist in June 1905. He wrote a thesis on coffee, *Les caféiers, structure anatomique de la feuille.* He took over his father's company in 1914. He died on December 1, 1935.

Angelo Mariani,
Father of Coca Wine

Marie-Anne Mariani (1846–78), wife of Angelo Mariani. Courtesy of E. Mariani.

The beginnings were difficult, as Mariani tells a journalist from *Le Figaro:*

Sometime before the siege of Paris, I had settled with my wife in a small apartment at 400 francs per year in the rue Vaneau. My only income at that time was my modest salary from being a pharmacy student, but thanks to the discovery that I had just made using coca leaves, I was full of confidence for the future. One day, the shelf, which was loosely attached to the wall and on which I had carefully

Angelo Mariani, Father of Coca Wine

put my first twelve liters of coca wine—which represented for me the beginning of fortune—fell down at my feet. The broken bottles spilled all of my precious coca![19]

Horror-stricken, he informed his wife of the disaster, and she advised him to start again: "The supportive trust of my wife gave me courage. I made some new savings; I bought a barrel of Bordeaux: I blended my next batch; the first bottles had an unexpected success. You know the rest."

Sometime later, Charles Fauvel, who had just moved into a building near the Opera House, still under construction, told Mariani that a small shop was vacant at 41 boulevard Haussmann. It was a brilliant idea, a perfect location, right next to the Opera, which was to be completed a few years later. The idea was that singers—future potential clients—would consult him before their vocal performances. Mariani established his own pharmacy in 1873 and began making his tonic wine. The first year he "made six thousand francs profit. The second year he doubled his income; and the total amount of the inventory for the third year was twenty-four thousand francs!"[20]

The Marianis left their small apartment on rue Vaneau, to settle at 11 rue Scribe, near his pharmacy.

On January 30, 1877, he created a company to develop his coca wine with a certain Jules Keisser, and on February 27 the company name was recorded in the commercial register.[21]

A few years later, Mariani would be indirectly behind the discovery of the anesthetic properties of the main alkaloid of coca, cocaine. The story is almost unknown.

According to his secretary, Mariani provided some cocaine for experimental purposes to Dr. Gabriel Coupard (1847–1912), the assistant of Dr. Fauvel, who, as noted above, was one of the first to discover the anesthetic properties of coca:

In 1880, after using coca extract [Dr. Coupard] had the idea to experiment with its alkaloid, cocaine. Mr. Mariani, who was the only one to possess it in France, was willing to offer him a small amount. Coupard's research on animals was done in the physiology

Dr. Gabriel Coupard
(1847–1912).

Angelo Mariani,
Father of Coca Wine

Advertising placard
for Vin Mariani, 1875.
Courtesy of E. Mariani.

Angelo Mariani,
Father of Coca Wine

Dr. Jean Baptiste Vincent Laborde
(1830–1903).

Dr. Karl Koller
(1857–1944).

Angelo Mariani,
Father of Coca Wine

laboratory of the Medical Faculty of Paris, directed by Dr. Laborde. Unfortunately, they were not published, although they undoubtedly showed the anesthetic action of cocaine. Therefore, four years later in 1884, when Koller announced the same discovery as his own, and when German newspapers made a great fuss about his paper, Dr. Laborde claimed on the rostrum before the Biology Society the priority of this important discovery for French science.[22]

In a paper to the Biology Society, the eminent physiologist Jean Baptiste Vincent Laborde (1830–1903) had indeed reported that:

Dr. Coupard had told us, on several occasions, about the repeatedly remarkable anesthetic properties of coca preparations. [...] In 1880, Coupard undertook [...] physiological experiments using a cocaine salt, [...] hydrochlorate.

The account in which he described one of these experiments showed, added Laborde, "the phenomena of general anesthesia and especially of ocular conjunctiva insensitivity" obtained by Coupard.

Dr. Laborde also mentioned his own work, already published in 1882, on the neutral sulphate of cocaine. He mentioned the work that Koller had just published, and concluded his paper by observing that:

The partial and localized anesthetic effects were discovered and were known long before the recent works, which, however, it is fair to say, have better defined the local action on the ocular conjunctiva, in order to draw the conclusions regarding application to ophthalmology surgery.[23]

It is indeed the famous Austrian ophthalmologist Karl Koller (1857–1944), put on the track by Freud, who is credited with the discovery of the anesthetic action of cocaine based on the paper about his research presented to the Medical Society of Vienna on October 17, 1884. He did not mention the works of the French doctors.

In a January 1885 article, the French correspondent of the great English medical journal the *Lancet* stated that the anesthetic properties of coca had been known long before Koller. The writings on the subject completely ignore, according to him, what was done in France in this field. He mentioned the works of Dr. Fauvel and of his two assistants, Dr. Scaglia and Dr. Coupard, and he expressed surprise that their research did not attract attention, either in their own country or elsewhere, before Koller.[24]

Many years later, the whole affair would be confirmed by the great surgeon Paul Reclus (1847–1914), who wrote in 1903:

> In 1877, Coupard observed on patients who were taking Mariani wine some anesthesia of the throat . . . and then, from 1882, with the assistance of Laborde, he studied, not coca anymore, but its alkaloid, cocaine. Unfortunately these researches were published after [Koller's] celebrated paper of 1884.[25]

Angelo Mariani,
Father of Coca Wine

3 Mariani's Laboratory and Its Coca-Based Products

Success, Innovation, and Expansion

Following the success of his wine, Mariani thought about expanding.

In 1884–85, he bought a 32,000-square-foot piece of land in Neuilly-sur-Seine (near Paris), at 10–12 rue de Chartres, where he set up his factory with an adjoining house and a large garden. The entire décor of

View of the Mariani factory.

Mariani's coca-themed
living room.

the house was a tribute to coca: "From the floor ornaments to the motifs
of the furniture, the tapestries on the walls, and the exquisite decorative
paintings."[1]

    He entrusted the décor of his living room, including the furniture, to
Saint André de Lignereux, and had Eugene Courboin paint an allegory
on the ceiling: *The Goddess Bringing a Branch of Coca to Europe.* Among
the different characters in this composition are a number of Mariani's first
friends: Madame Fauvel, Armand Silvestre, and Charles Gounod.[2]

    Attached to the house Mariani built two greenhouses, one of

Mariani's Laboratory
and Its Coca-Based
Products

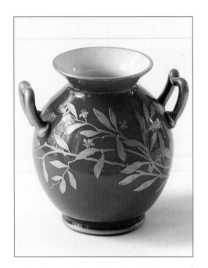

Red vase from Mariani's home. Coca leaves comprise the design. Courtesy of E. Mariani.

Decanter and glass from Mariani's home. Coca leaves were incorporated into the design, as they were for many items in his home. Courtesy of E. Mariani.

Mariani's Laboratory and Its Coca-Based Products

375 square feet, the other 270 square feet, where Mariani cultivated coca plants for his pleasure: "I saw coca plants there, grown from seed or by cuttings, which, a few years old, were already almost two meters high."[3]

An American visitor, Dr. William Golden Mortimer (1854–1933), member of the Academy of Medicine and editor of the *Pharmaceutical Journal* and of the *New York Journal of Medicine,* once visited Mariani's factory in Neuilly because he wanted to publish a detailed study of the history of coca. His book, published in 1901, still considered one of the best studies on the subject, was dedicated to his friend Angelo Mariani: "a recognized exponent of the divine plant and the first to render coca available to the world." He described the greenhouses, "filled with thousands of coca plants of various species, among which he takes the greatest delight in experimenting upon peculiarities of growth and on cultivation. From his collection specimen plants have been freely distributed to botanical gardens in all parts of the world."[4]

A reporter from *Le Figaro* described the factory, for its part, that was in the basement, with its

> model workshops, extensive cellars, bright and meticulously clean, in which wagons loaded with bottles circulate noiselessly, and where an elite group of experienced and devoted workers operate under the eye of the master; the accomplishment of this constant work is aided by very modern and sophisticated equipment, almost elegant—such is the house.[5]

The factory consisted of seven rooms, each dedicated to a different function: a washroom for the bottles, a vat room, a barrel room, a room for storing the empty bottles, a room for storing the filled bottles, a room for packing and labeling the crates, and a room for crate storage. According to the only description available of the equipment used to manufacture Mariani's products, we learn that in 1904 it consisted of:

> Two engines producing five horsepower, three copper tanks, one containing 3,000 liters of wine, the other two containing 2,000 liters each, the first, for the elixir, and the second for the mixture; finally 25 devices for maceration and 32 wooden vats, each containing 1,500 liters of wine ready to bottle.[6]

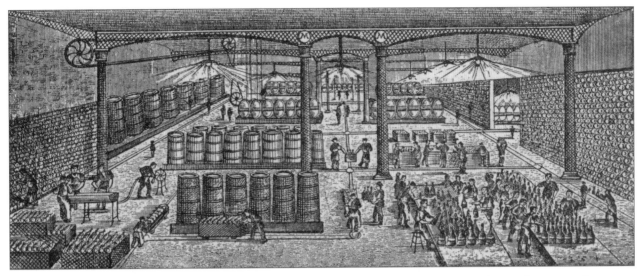

Cellars at the Mariani factory.

Mariani was one of the first in France to institute the "English week" for the eighteen employees of his factory. One of his workers remarked, "Good boss, he did not wait to be asked, he offered it."[7]

In the factory, precision and attention to detail reigned supreme:

> Up to and including rinsing the bottles, through the laboratory, the racking devices, the huge tanks, the whole a precious and expert process, where nothing is left to chance, and where the most meticulous precautions are systematically taken for the greater perfection of the work and greater satisfaction of the customer. One detail—among a hundred—which seems to be nothing, and yet tells a lot about the method [. . .] the label of each bottle bears a cabalistic number, usually consisting of five or six digits. [. . .] This is a mnemonic code so that, in the event that a buyer complained of having been badly served, the cuvée that was the source of the offending bottle could be identified. The racking of each vintage had its own serial number, representing all the factors in the operation.[8]

Such care made it possible to avoid any risk of error, and this attention to detail reassured the consumers about the quality of the products. In the laboratory, Dr. Mortimer stated:

> There is no secret other than method claimed in the process which has made the name of its inventor synonymous with that of Coca,

Doctor William Golden Mortimer (1854–1933).

Mariani's Laboratory and Its Coca-Based Products

39

Preparation of Vin Mariani.

though I heard an anecdote related of this gentleman, who personally scrutinizes every detail of manufacture, that: "after everything else is done he goes around and drops something else in." Whether this be so or not, it is certain that the preparations of Coca manufactured by Mariani are entirely different in aroma and action from other Coca preparations which I have examined. These latter have not the agreeable flavor of Coca, but the fluid extracts are usually bitter and the wines have a peculiar birch-like taste comparable with the smell of an imitation Russia leather.[9]

It was from this factory, which would become the largest in the world for coca preparations, that Mariani's famous Tonic Wine with Coca from Peru, more commonly called Vin Mariani, would spread all over the world. The journalist Émile Gautier described the characteristics of the wine in these terms:

Nothing is more French, more marked with the character of the terroir and the race, than this Gallic liqueur whose flow of gold and purple, retains, mixed with the warm aroma of tropical vegetation,

Mariani's Laboratory and Its Coca-Based Products

Rinsing the bottles.

I know not what perfume of elegance, nobility, chivalry, and sweetness.[10]

According to Mariani:

The wine contains the soluble parts of the Peruvian plant. The combination of coca with the tannin and the slight traces of iron naturally contained in Bordeaux wine make for the most efficacious of tonics. The coca leaves that we employ come from three different sources and are of incomparable quality.[11]

Mariani's experimentation, said Dr. Mortimer, "led to combining several varieties of leaf, setting aside those which contained chiefly the bitter principle—since known to be cocaine—and selecting those which contained the aromatic alkaloids."[12]

The question of the origin of the coca leaves he used is complex and must have varied at different times. Mariani said, in an article he published

Vin Mariani label.

Mariani's Laboratory and Its Coca-Based Products

Bottling of Vin Mariani.

in 1875, that the leaves he used "were collected on one of the most exposed slopes of Bolivia." In his later writings, in particular in 1904, he favored, he said, leaves from Peru, sweeter and less bitter than those of Bolivia, which were used primarily in the production of cocaine. It is likely that Mariani used Bolivian coca leaves only in the early stages of his company, then used several varieties of only Peruvian coca leaves to make a blend to improve his preparation.

In 1907, his secretary Joseph Uzanne offered interesting testimony: "At the beginning, we had to run all the wholesale druggists of the Marais to be able to gather a lousy kilo of the precious leaf. Today, it comes from Peru by the boatload."

According to an official study published by the Directorate of Departmental Affairs of the Seine (Paris), by that year, Mariani's laboratory was importing between twelve and fifteen tons of coca leaves annually from Peru.[13]

The preparation of Vin Mariani varied as well. In 1875, Mariani gave the only existing detailed description of the method employed:

We prepare our wine by draining off coca leaves mixed with their *llipta* [lime] using brandy at 61 percent and adding the amount of 60 grams of leaves to 1,000 grams of sweet wine containing 23 percent

Wrapping the bottles.

View of the entrance to the Mariani factory.

alcohol. This wine contains the amount of alcohol required to dissolve the cocaine and the excess of water sufficient to hold in solution the ecgonine [coca alkaloid] and the gummy principles of the leaf.[14]

The preparation appears to have been subsequently modified. Mariani replaced the sweet wine with a Bordeaux (maison Henry Clausel).

Mariani's Laboratory
and Its Coca-Based
Products

Advertising card for Vin Mariani.

For the fluid extract of coca, Mariani was probably starting by reducing to powder 60 grams of coca leaves using a grinder. This powder was then transferred to a rotary percolator to macerate in alcohol (brandy), which dissolved the constituents of the coca leaves. The result obtained by percolation was then incorporated into the Bordeaux by adding glycerin mixed with an acidifier and about 6 percent sugar. The final product titrated between 14 and 17 percent alcohol according to the analyses. This rate is explained, in our opinion, by the chaptalization obtained by the addition of sugar.[15]

The use of Vin Mariani quickly became fashionable. The name of the propagator of coca was even used as a verb by a member of the Academy of Medicine. It was reported that an enthusiastic lover of this wine and its healing power against the flu exclaimed: "Let us Marianize, it is the safeguard!"[16]

In 1901, the magazine *La Couturière* presented a dress for ladies called the Vicuna Mariani.[17] A candy called Gismonda, made with Vinay chocolate and Vin Mariani, was sold in grocery stores in Paris.[18]

In the United States and Canada one could find the Mariani cocktail: half a wine glass of Vin Mariani, a quarter of vermouth, a few drops of angostura, a half teaspoon of curaçao, and lemon zest, all mixed in a shaker with crushed ice.[19]

Mariani received numerous awards: an honorary diploma at the Bordeaux Wine Fair, the gold medal and honorary diploma at the Hygienic Exhibition in Amsterdam, and the gold medal and diploma in Leamington (UK), in which the jury described his wine as "the Wine of Athletes."

According to the testimony of Dr. Lelong, author of a study on the therapeutic properties of coca:

> In the days of great parliamentary struggles, our honorable members of Parliament have recourse to Vin Mariani, which is well stocked in the bar of the Chamber of Deputies. The night of their premières our great singers in the National Academy of Music and the Comic Opera always have a few bottles of Vin Mariani in their dressing room, and their repeated testimonials told us that with this precious liqueur they had been constantly protected from the vocal accidents so common on the stage.[20]

Types of Vin Mariani bottles.

VIN TONIQUE MARIANI

A LA

COCA DU PEROU

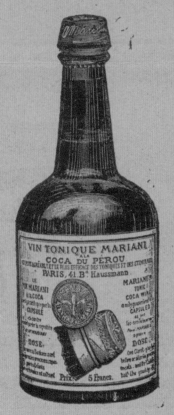

Le plus agréable

le plus efficace

DES TONIQUES

ET

DES STIMULANTS

———

Exiger la capsule verte et la signature de M. Mariani

———

PARIS, 41, Boulevard Haussmann.

NEW-YORK : 52, West, 15th Street.

Et toutes les pharmacies

Vin Mariani advertising insert.

The only figures available show that, by 1906, an estimated 10 million bottles had been sold.[21] In 1904, annual production was 800,000 or 900,000 bottles, with 90 percent sold in France and the other 10 percent abroad.[22]

"Allow any quantity of Coca Mariani for the president, but not too much for members of Parliament."
—Paul Deschanel, president of the Republic; *Albums Mariani*, vol. 5

Other Coca Specialty Products

In addition to wine, Mariani produced other preparations of coca—tea, elixir, paste, lozenges, and a liqueur.

- *Thé Mariani* (Mariani Tea), or concentrated extract of coca, was eight times more potent than Vin Mariani. It was a drink made with 10 grams of coca in 6.5 fluid ounces of water, highly recommended for "persons who climb mountains or go on fatiguing marches or long journeys through unhealthy countries." The prescribed dose was 1 or 3 teaspoons three or four times a day, pure or mixed with water, milk, brandy, or wine. It was sold in 4-ounce bottles and came in a cardboard box. The cost was $1.50 per bottle.

- *Elixir Mariani* contained more alcohol and three times as much of the active principles of the coca leaf as Vin Mariani. It was made of a mixture of 100 grams of coca leaves in powder with 150 grams of brandy, 180 grams of sugar, filtered and marketed in half-liter bottles. It contained 36.3 percent alcohol and 0.025 percent alkaloids. The prescribed dose as a liqueur was a glassful after main meals. It could be taken pure or mixed with cold water, in the proportions of two liqueur glasses to a tumbler of water, which made for a fortifying and pleasant drink. The cost was $1.50 per bottle.

- *Pâte Mariani* was a coca-based "tonic and pectoral" paste made "with equal parts infusion and tincture [of coca] added to sweet gum. The mass is evaporated and divided into small oval pieces about the size of a bean that are then candied." The lozenges were used to cure obstinate coughs, sore throats, and other respiratory disorders. The product was especially recommended for speakers, singers, teachers, and those in other professions where the vocal organs could be strained. The prescribed dose was 6 to 10 lozenges a day. They were sold in an enamel tin containing 60 tablets and cost $1.00 per box.

Illustration by Augustin Poupart (18?–19?) from the coca tale *Cypselos l'invincible* (Cypselos the invincible), 1904. Angelo Mariani's initials and often-used symbols of the coca leaf and cherub are seen.

Mariani's Laboratory and Its Coca-Based Products

Tin box of Pâte Mariani.

🖎 *Pastilles Mariani,* "analgesic, tonic, and pectoral" lozenges, were meant to be used for the same conditions as *Pâte Mariani,* from which they differed only by the addition of 2 milligrams of cocaine hydrochlorate to each pastille. Their action was much more intense and more rapid than that of the coca paste. The prescribed dose was 4 to 8 daily. They were sold in an enamel tin containing 30 tablets at a cost of $1.00 per box.

🖎 *Mariani Extract* allowed one to make one's own coca wine. A bottle of the extract cost $3.00 and contained enough to turn five bottles of commercial wine into coca wine.

There were other preparations from the catalog of Mariani specialties that met with less success.

🖎 *Terpine Mariani* was a liqueur that combined the anticatarrhal properties of terpine hydrate upon mucous membranes with the general tonic and beneficial action of coca. Each tablespoonful contained 20 centigrams of terpine. The prescribed dose was 1 or 2 teaspoons every two to three hours to relieve cough and bronchial

Drawing by Felix Hippolyte Lucas (1854–1925). Courtesy of E. Mariani.

congestion, or 1 tablespoon three to four times a day before meals and before bedtime as a respiratory stimulant. It was to be taken with or without water and a bottle cost $1.50. It still existed in 1962.

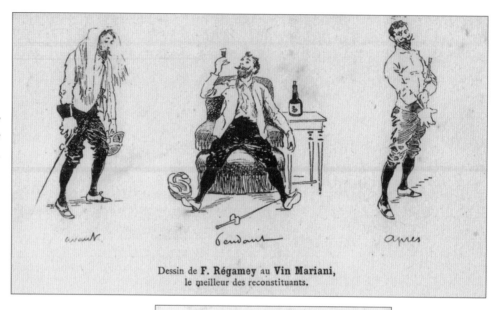

Postcard by Félix Régamey (1844–1907).

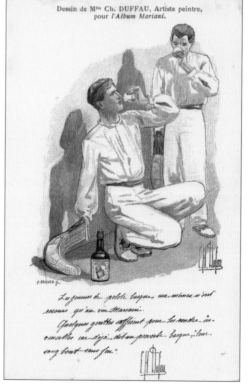

Postcard by Clémentine-Hélène Dufau (1869–1937).

- *Pepsi-Coca Mariani* was a preparation containing pepsin and coca.
- *Vélo-coca Mariani* (Mariani Bike Coca). Mariani said in regard to this product that many champion cyclists sought him out "in the hope of getting [. . .] the wonderful product that will give them the energy needed to keep their strength up on long journeys." He added: "We immediately put at the disposal of the cyclists our Vélo-coca, a concentrated coca preparation, which could be preserved indefinitely and easily transported in small amounts."[23]

Watercolor by Georges Meunier (1869–1942). Courtesy of galerie Christian Pons.

Mariani's products were indeed very popular among sportsmen of all kinds, and there are some eloquent testimonials in the *Albums*, mainly from aviators, among them Louis Blériot and Alberto Santos-Dumont. A sports magazine of the time called *La vie au grand air* (Outdoor Life) published in one of its numbers a double page of testimonials from cyclists, riders, shooters, runners, motor racers, fencers, boxers, and wrestlers—all lovers of Vin Mariani.[24]

Dr. Lelong finds that:

These [. . .] preparations, which now bear his name, have penetrated all classes of European society; everywhere from the city to the smallest village, women, children, convalescents of all ages now know the name of the beneficial plant that the sacrifices of Mariani have popularized, and all those who suffer owe him some benefit.[25]

4 The Medicinal Virtues of Vin Mariani

The Story of Coca in the United States and France

In the United States

Angelo Mariani quickly became very famous and saw his products distributed almost everywhere in the world. The company soon had branches in the capitals of a half dozen European countries as well as in Buenos Aires, Colombo, Shanghai, Saigon, and Alexandria.

Postcard, 1900.

Mariani wanted to expand his business in North America. He first opened an office in Montreal and then one in New York. In 1880, the New York office was located at 50 Exchange Place, and in 1886 at 127 Fifth Avenue. In 1889, he moved his office to 52 West 15th Street. In 1932 the office was still at the same address according to the *Supplément illustré* (28th series) advertising insert published by the Mariani company.

Illustration with inscription by GASTON GÉRARD, Artist painter. (From the Album Mariani, Paris, France).

"Glory to the Wine Tonic Mariani."

VIN MARIANI Ideal Appetizer and Tonic-Stimulant, at Grocers and Wine Merchants. Try a VIN MARIANI Cocktail at Hotels, Bars and Cafés.

An American postcard for Vin Mariani, illustrated by Gaston Gérard (1859–?).

It was the tragic story of President Grant that made Mariani's wine famous in the United States. In the summer of 1884, Grant began to suffer from terminal throat cancer. Wishing to leave money to his family, he decided to write his memoirs. His doctors administered Mariani Tea or Vin Mariani to him, which relieved his pain and nourished him when he could no longer eat. In doing so they were able to extend the life of their illustrious patient for a few months so he could finish writing his memoirs, completed just a few days before his death in the summer of 1885. Americans became impassioned by the story of Grant's race against death.

Mariani became a kind of national hero. He came to New York in 1885, according to a U.S. pharmaceutical magazine, at the request of a number of prominent physicians who desired to get from him personally a better understanding of the nature, preparation, and administration of this wonderful medicine. In the case of General Grant, the physicians have found the merits of Vin Mariani to be all they could have expected.[1]

A publication by Mariani & Co. gives more details:

Former president Grant was dying. [. . .] Arriving the day before in New York, Mariani was stopped by the silent crowd blocking

Postcard, 1900.

Other companies would soon adopt Mariani's advertising methods and tout the medical benefits of their products, as seen in this advertisement for Vin du docteur Clément.

the traffic and preventing cars from passing in front of the house. Confident in the wonderful virtues of coca that he had revealed to scientists in Europe, he wanted to propose that the physicians try an experiment that could be beneficial. Having passed his card to Dr. Douglas, Mariani was admitted, and a few moments later, a teaspoon of extract of coca mixed with a sip of milk was introduced to the inert lips of the dying. To the surprise of doctors, this drink was kept down, and the ensuing light slumber gave them hope that the work of death was suspended. Two or three such doses were administered during the evening, and similarly tolerated by the stomach. A quiet night followed this day of anxieties. Always mixed with milk, the extract of coca Mariani continued to be tolerated and digested, and under the active virtue of this sacrament, the slow awakening of the functions became more consoling, more decisive. For three months, always supported and nourished with the milk mixed with coca, the hero defended himself thanks to the comforting beverage.[2]

Mariani stated that personal physicians of General Grant have

authorized us to bring to make known that it was due to *Thé Mariani,* added to milk (in the proportion of a teaspoonful of *Thé* to a cup of milk), that they were able to nourish General Grant, the ex-President, when he was unable to support any other food. By this means they succeeded in prolonging the life of their illustrious patient for several months.[3]

Mariani's brother-in-law and partner Julius Jaros (1856–1925) undertook the management and promotion of Mariani products in the United States.

Mariani published several monographs on coca and Vin Mariani in the United States, which contained, among other things, excerpts of French and American medical articles and testimonials of doctors advocating his products.

In one of his monographs, *Coca and Its Therapeutic Application* (1890), he published a list of 2,880 names of American physicians, "Who have been good enough to formally endorse Vin Mariani, their experience in prescribing in hospital and private practice having caused them to believe the preparation valuable and reliable."[4]

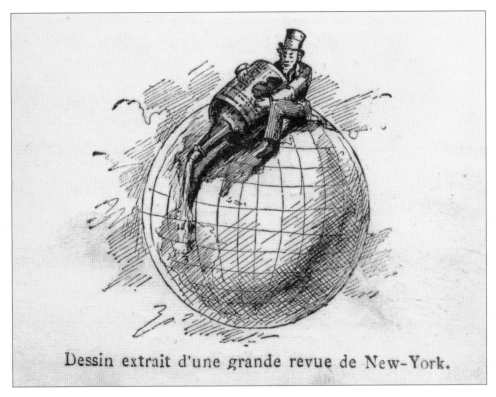

Dessin extrait d'une grande revue de New-York.

Drawing from a New York magazine, in *Supplément illustré*, 1902.

Another of his monographs, *The Efficacy of Coca Erythroxylon: Notes and Comments by Prominent Physicians* (2nd edition, 1889), provided the geographical origin of these endorsements. Thirty-five states and the District of Columbia are represented, indicating a nationwide distribution system. Approximatively 650 names are from New York State (the book gives excerpts of around 130 of their letters). The second most represented state is Pennsylvania with around 230 names (and 25 excerpts). The third state is Ohio with nearly 100 names (and 9 excerpts). The fourth most represented state is Massachusetts with around 90 names (and 11 excerpts).

Among these medical endorsers, we can mention the father of spinal anesthesia, Dr. Leonard Corning, who wrote in 1884 that "the preparation of coca known as Mariani's Coca Wine is, so far as I know, the best in the market. It possesses the decided advantage of being manufactured from fresh leaves, which is an indispensable requisite." He recommended it in cases of depression.

In his book, the health commissioner of New York City, Dr. Cyrus Edson, recommended Vin Mariani as hot grog to cure influenza.

The Medicinal Virtues
of Vin Mariani

Dessin

de

M. MAUROU,

Artiste lithographe,

pour

l'Album Mariani.

Postcard by Paul Maurou
(1848–1931).

A professor of clinical medicine at Bellevue Hospital in New York, Beverley Robinson, recommended its use as a heart tonic, because of the excellent quality of the coca leaves.

Dr. Charles Sajous, a throat doctor and endocrinologist, recommended coca wine for cases of hoarseness in professional singers. The one he recommended was Vin Mariani, which, unlike other "coca wines on the market [which], are but solutions of cocaine," possessed only an "infinitesimal amount" and did not cause constipation. "It can for that reason be administered continuously [. . .] in cases in which muscular weakness causes tremulousness of the voice."[5]

In another of his booklets, *Contemporary Celebrities* (1901), Mariani claimed to have received eight thousand letters from eminent physicians all over the world. The advertisements published in the same period mention that eight thousand American physicians had endorsed Vin Mariani.

The Medicinal Virtues
of Vin Mariani

Postcard depicting
Dr. Dupont pouring Vin
Mariani in Senegal.

Mariani could have had an illustrious predecessor in the United States in the person of Mark Twain, who in his youth thought of getting rich with coca. In his autobiography he related that in 1856 he decided to emigrate to Brazil and become a coca farmer. "I was fired with a longing to ascend the Amazon. Also with a longing to open up a trade in coca with all the world."[6]

Despite this, coca and its therapeutic uses raised very little interest in the United States in the fifteen years following 1859 (the year when Albert Niemann isolated cocaine), perhaps due to the fact that the coca leaves would have lost their active properties during transport to the United States and were said to be of a low quality. Except for a first article in 1861, and a second in 1870, it would take until 1876–77 for the first medical articles to appear.[7] The number would increase starting in 1880 with the creation of *The Therapeutic Gazette* by the Parke, Davis & Company laboratories in

"Your coca from America, gives to my 'White Fathers,' sons of Europe, the courage and strength to civilize Asia and Africa." —Cardinal Lavigerie; *Albums Mariani*, vol. 1

The Medicinal Virtues
of Vin Mariani

Detroit. The journal would publish about twenty articles on coca between 1880 and 1884 alone. These articles would be one of Sigmund Freud's most important sources for the writing of his 1884 article "Über Coca." Before it became the major laboratory for the production and sale of cocaine, Parke, Davis & Co. offered six coca-based products in its 1885 catalog: a fluid extract of coca, coca wine, coca liqueur, coca cheroots, coca cigarettes (for respiratory ailments), and a 5 percent coca oil (for treating neuralgia). In its pamphlet, Parke, Davis proclaimed coca:

> A drug which through its stimulant properties, can supply the place of food, make the coward brave, the silent eloquent, free the victims of alcohol and opium habit from their bondage, and, as an anaesthetic render the sufferer insensitive to pain, and make attainable to the surgeon heights of what may be termed, 'aesthetic surgery' never reached before.[8]

One of the first therapeutic indications of coca that was put forward in many of these articles of *The Therapeutic Gazette* was for the treatment of addiction to opium and alcoholism.[9] William S. Searle, a physician from New York, was most likely one of the first American physicians to advocate the use of coca chewing or infusions. In a paper read in May 1880 before the Medico-Chirurgical Society of New York, he mentioned that his interest in this plant started during a trip to Peru in 1865. After his return he regularly imported coca leaves, which he first used on himself and then, starting in 1879, gave to his patients to treat nervous afflictions. He noted that, "Nearly all, the leaves and extracts which are on the market at present, are entirely worthless" and that there are only two places in New York where one can find "good Coca" and "fine extract." He reported that he had used coca:

> For business men who are kept by the pressure of business from their noonday meal, and who, too frequently, resort to alcoholic stimulus to tide them through the rush of the day, and all testify to its sustaining power not only, but claim its superiority to alcohol, in that they experience no reaction from its primary effects.

He looked to coca as "the great preserver of life and health in future generations," and concluded his paper by saying, "The introduction of

Vin Bravais poster, 1893, by Eugène Ogé (1861–1936). The words strength, health, vigor, and beauty are associated with the product. Courtesy of J. Santo Domingo.

this substance into general use is a matter of exceeding importance, and its employment should be fostered by every true physician."[10]

The recommended mode of administration in the first articles was the traditional Indian way, namely, chewing the leaves. Then came the infusion or fluid extract of coca, followed by coca leaves for smoking and coca wine, which we will study more thoroughly in chapter 7. The fluid extract of coca was admitted to the *U.S. Pharmacopoeia* in 1882, the coca wine in 1905.

As already mentioned, coca leaves were also used for smoking. In 1876 in a letter to the editor of the *Lancet,* Louis Lewis, a doctor from Philadelphia, stated that he was prescribing coca leaves for smoking in cases of idiopathic asthma and in chronic irritating cough.[11] Another doctor from the same city, Francis E. Stewart, reported in 1885 that he prescribed coca cigars, that he manufactured himself, for patients with hay fever. In 1885, he published the results of his research and experiments in an article of the *Philadelphia Medical Times* in which he noted the antidepressant and stimulant effects of smoking coca leaves as well as its exhilarating effects.[12] The same year a Saint Louis company, Cocabacco, launched Cocarettes, which were cigarettes made of tobacco and coca leaves rolled in French rice paper.

American coca imports exploded between 1884 and 1906, rising from around 25 tons to 1,300 tons.[13]

From 1897 to 1900, the American historian of coca Dr. William Golden Mortimer carried out a major investigation, probably the only one ever done, on the use of coca by U.S. doctors. He sent out 10,000 letters

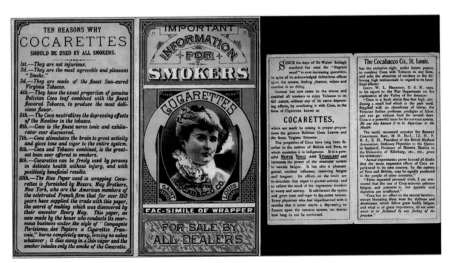

Advertisement for Cocarettes.

The Medicinal Virtues
of Vin Mariani

asking doctors for the results of their own observations on the use of coca. He received 1,206 responses. Among them, only 44 doctors said they did not obtain results, while 369 gave precise information on its physiological action and therapeutic applications. The numbers were as follows:

1. Physiological actions: strengthened heart, 117; increased appetite, 113 (diminished 27); stimulated the mind, 109; stimulated circulation, 107; improved digestive functions, 104; raised blood pressure, 88; improved nutrition, 85; strengthened muscles, 82; stimulated sexual functions, 60 (lowered 4); stimulated nerves, 58 (sedated 21); improved sleep, 58 (prevented 30); increased respiration, 40.
2. Therapeutic applications: debility, 141; exhaustion, 133; neurasthenia, 124; overwork, 106; alcoholism, 85; sexual exhaustion, 77; flu, 77; nutrition, 66; nerves, 65; melancholia, 64; anemia, 59; voice, 58; muscle, 55; brain, 49; stomach, 43; fever, 42; heart, 42; lungs, 32; asthma, 30; throat 29; bronchitis, 23.
3. In the survey, 167 doctors stated that coca did not lead to addiction (21 said it did).
4. Of the respondents, 276 doctors specified the form of coca they used. Of these, 229 had used coca wine. A large majority of them used Vin Mariani.[14]

From 1902 to 1906 Mariani published a quarterly magazine in New York called *Mariani's Coca Leaf* (1902–06), which was distributed free to some 50,000 doctors. It was a small sixteen-page brochure dedicated to presenting "the most recent facts concerning the application of coca to the various uses for which it is recommended." It also published articles on general medicine.

The Mariani name became known to all. People wrote him from around the world. Most letters came from doctors praising the properties of his wine.

One such letter came from Hot Springs, Arkansas, and was signed "H. Torney, Surgeon General, Hospital of the Army and the Navy":

A large quantity of Vin Mariani was used on the hospital ship of the United States *The Relief,* and we recognized that this wine was of great value in the care of the sick among the troops in Cuba and

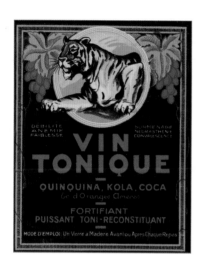

Label of a French tonic coca wine promising strength to the consumer.

The Medicinal Virtues of Vin Mariani

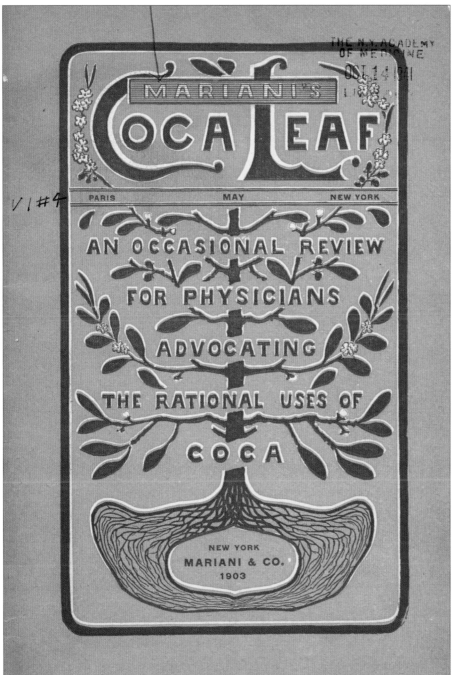

Cover of *Mariani's Coca Leaf* magazine.

Puerto Rico and for those who were sent by boat to be repatriated to the United States. Many people were debilitated by fever and extreme heat and have found in your excellent wine a powerful restorative and an unrivalled tonic.[15]

In France

Unlike in the United States, coca and its therapeutic uses elicited numerous articles and theses in France after 1859, the year when Albert Niemann isolated cocaine. In the twenty years that followed, at least a dozen articles, five theses, and seven monographs were devoted to coca. Mariani had certainly played a role in this interest in the sacred plant; doctors often mentioned his name and his coca products in their articles on coca.

In his own publications, Mariani said that his wine had medicinal properties and could be prescribed in the following cases: "The flu, influenza, nerve disorders, stomach aches, anemia, fever, insomnia, chest diseases, overwork, neurasthenia, convalescence, blood loss, impotence, melancholy, the weakening of the brain, diseases of the throat and lungs, epidemics and contagious diseases, nervous prostration, and finally, general debility."

Postcard by Evert van Muyden (1853–1922).

His coca wine was on the tip of everyone's lips, so much so that after the 1889 influenza outbreak in Paris, his wine was one of the most highly recommended drugs. Charles Fauvel even humorously christened it "the lightning rod of the flu" when it was used in the form of a grog by mixing it with hot water and sugar.[16]

Dr. Lieberman, surgeon-in-chief of the French army, told Mariani that he used his wine:

The Medicinal Virtues
of Vin Mariani

With great success for profound anemia resulting from long and tedious campaigns in hot countries, and accompanied, as is nearly always the case, by gastrointestinal irritation with loss of appetite and dyspepsia. [. . .] I have also employed it in cases, happily rare in our army, of chronic alcoholism, resulting from the abuse of brandy, absinthe or strong liquors. [. . .] I have frequently seen hardened drinkers renounce their fatal habit and return to a healthy condition. I have also used Vin Mariani to save smokers of exaggerated habits, from nicotinism. [. . .] I have also employed it with success for chronic bronchitis and pulmonary phthisis. Vin Mariani increases the appetite and diminishes the cough in these two morbid states. [. . .] Besides I have used it to the greatest advantage in convalescence from typhoid fever, when no wine, not even Bordeaux, was retained by the stomach on account of gastric irritation which is the rule after fevers of this nature. [. . .] I can certify that Vin Mariani is the most powerful weapon that can be put in the hands of military physicians to combat the diseases, the infirmities, and even the vicious habits engendered by camp life and the servitude of military existence.[17]

Dr. Villeneuve, for his part, talks about one of his patients, a lawyer who had become addicted to morphine used to treat his severe chronic bronchitis. He reported the following observation to Mariani:

When I commenced to treat the patient, he was taking daily from 1 gramme 50 centigrammes to 1 gramme 80 centigrammes [1.5 to 1.8 grams] of morphine hypodermically. [. . .] After a month of treatment, I had succeeded to reduce the daily doses. [. . .] However, the congestion and especially the dyspepsia was very grave, and the cough which had been suppressed by morphine came back again. It was then that I treated my patient with phosphate of lime, the *Pâte* and the Vin Mariani. Lacking his habitual stimulant, he was plunged in a semi-coma. [. . .] But in about a week, during which he took 10 doses of *Pâte de Coca* daily, the cough became less fatiguing and disappeared entirely in about twenty days. The patient then commenced to take small doses of Vin Mariani. [. . .] Now he can go and take his dinner in town, [. . .] is able to undertake anew his occupations, and has entirely given up his morphine habit.[18]

Vin Désiles poster, 1895, by Francisco Tamagno (1851–1933). Courtesy of J. Santo Domingo.

The Medicinal Virtues of Vin Mariani

"Jeunesse" Engraving by
Albert Robida (1848–1926).

Dr. Charles Gazeau, whose medical thesis (1870), quoted by Freud, was called *Nouvelles recherches expérimentales sur la pharmacologie, la physiologie et la thérapeutique du coca* (New Experimental Researches on the Pharmacology, Physiology, and Therapeutics of Coca) mentioned, in an 1872 article called "Observations on the Uses of Coca," the case of one of his syphilitic patients who had lost his appetite and was having pain

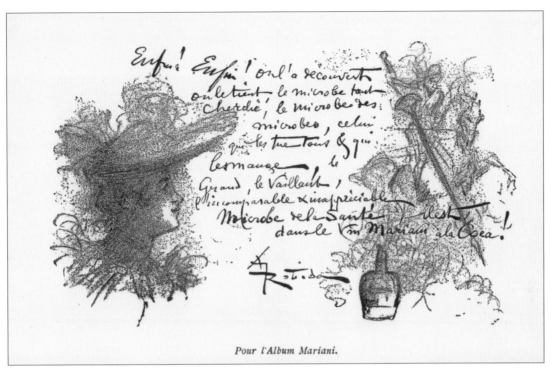

Pour l'Album Mariani.

Postcard by Albert Robida
(1848–1926).

and difficulty digesting food. He gave him a glass of Vin Mariani and 0.50 grams of coca powder a quarter hour before meals. After three weeks, he found that the patient's digestive functions were restored and his energy revived. "The coca appeared to be eupeptic and frankly tonic."[19]

In an 1877 article published in *La gazette des hôpitaux* on therapeutic applications of coca, Dr. Joseph Scaglia believed coca was supreme for treating:

> Anemia, connected with chronic pulmonary affections, in anemia accompanied by gastralgia. [. . .] [But also in the case of] cerebral weakness due to excess work or pleasure, the exhaustion from which the inhabitants of large cities suffer through irregularities of diet and imperfect hygiene owing to their surroundings.[20]

He named various Mariani preparations that "were executed with such perfection, that we can say that it greatly contributed to the popularization of coca."

Dr. Nitard, in another article of the same year in the same journal, observed that Vin Mariani:

The Medicinal Virtues
of Vin Mariani

Postcard, ca. 1910, by Hippolyte Berteaux (1843–1926). Beneath the image the text reads, "Vin Mariani is unsurpassed for convalescence."

"Politicians should be at the forefront of those who sing the praises of Vin Mariani. No profession requires tonic and comforting more than theirs." —Albert Lebrun, president of the Republic; *Supplément illustré*, 1932

The Medicinal Virtues of Vin Mariani

Succeeds where others preparations have failed, stimulating, on the one hand, by the small amount of tannin it contains, the functions of the stomach; while on the other hand, the active principles of coca, carried along with the alcohol that serves as their vehicle, will excite the vitality of every organ separately, but not without having previously exercised their vivifying action on the gastric mucosa itself.[21]

Dr. P. Collin, in an article also from 1877, published in *L'union médicale* and mentioned by Freud, believed that:

Of all the pharmaceutical coca-based preparations, we must mention more particularly the wine offered by Mr. Mariani. This skillful chemist was able to dissolve the active principles of the coca in a Bordeaux wine. [. . .] [His different preparations] act in a special and masterly way to treat granular pharyngitis, tonsillary angina, albuminuria, and diabetes, and their stimulating properties on the nervous cerebrospinal system cannot be ignored.[22]

Dr. M. Odin reported that in 1882 he admitted an anorexic and depressed woman in a state of general weakness, "after having tried all the treatments in vain." He decided to administer her Vin Mariani at the usual doses. He noted that:

After eight days the improvement is significant, the lack of appetite is gone, the taking nourishment becomes possible, and the digestive functions are regularized [. . .]. After one month of treatment the situation is most satisfactory.[23]

Over the years, the daily newspapers multiplied the articles on Mariani's products and their therapeutic properties.

In 1901, *Le Figaro* reported that Li Hung-chang (1823–1901), a Chinese general and politician, was able to keep alive and in good shape during his last years thanks to Vin Mariani. He recommended it to his sovereign, the emperor of China who, being at the point of death, had with "great success, made a cure of this wine, after which his life was prolonged despite fatigue and melancholy."[24]

In 1909, *Le Figaro* reported that the American explorer Robert

Watercolor by Henri Boutet (1851–1919). Beneath the image the text reads, "Vin Mariani gives rosy cheeks to the baby whose mother takes it."

E. Peary (1856–1920), during his expedition to the North Pole, had taken the precaution of bringing along several cases of Vin Mariani.[25]

In 1913, during the First Balkan War, *Le Figaro* kept its readers informed of the receipt by the French hospital in Constantinople, as well

The Medicinal Virtues of Vin Mariani

Postcard depicting a nun giving Vin Mariani to a wounded soldier.

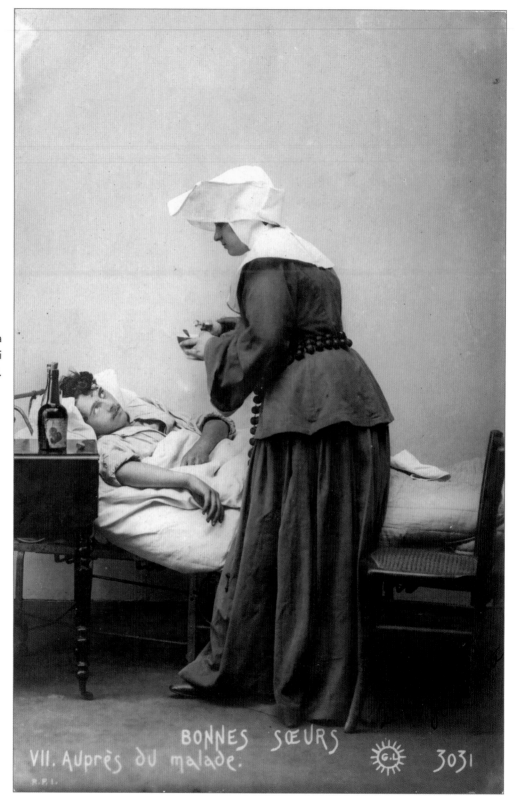

BONNES SŒURS

VII. Auprès du malade.

3031

as by the hospitals of different warring parties, of cases of Vin Mariani intended to treat the wounded. The wife of the ambassador of France thanks Mariani in these terms:

> You would not believe how precious your shipment of wine is. Whether it is our exhausted nuns or our poor disabled, all, like myself, thank you for your generosity.[26]

Some consumers used or abused Vin Mariani. Among them, according to various accounts, was the famous French novelist Pierre Louÿs (1870–1925) at the end of his life. According to his friend, the writer Paul Léautaud:

> For several years, Louÿs had not left home. For several months, he lived in his bed, feeding on liquids: a daily average of two bottles of champagne, three bottles of wine, one bottle of Mariani. In addition, morphine and cocaine. The result was predictable.[27]

Another testimonial goes further:

> He spent his nights awake, slept once every three days, drank Vin Mariani at incredible doses, three to four bottles a day, smoked sixty to eighty cigarettes in twenty-four hours, not to mention the use of some conventional poisons.[28]

What we do not know was whether this energetic treatment allowed him to live a bit longer or if it accelerated his death.

5 The Father of Modern Advertising

······················

From the *Albums Mariani* to Patronage of the Arts

Despite the growing success of his products and the laudatory testimonials of the doctors, Mariani and his wine probably would not have met with their immense fame without his exceptional talent for advertising. Mariani quickly realized that advertising was crucial to publicizing his wine worldwide. Until Mariani, the usual way of doing business was to surround oneself with loyal customers. If the product was good, word of mouth would do the rest. Mariani was interested in finding a new way to advertise. He did not want to start a traditional advertising campaign by displaying the name of his company on every available wall, or by placing an advertisement in all the magazines and newspapers. If he did, he would have found himself mixed in with charlatans hawking preparations for making hair grow instantly on a bald head, or for prolonging youth, and whatnot.

Marcel Bleustein-Blanchet, who founded the well-known advertising agency Publicis in 1927, reported that in his youth:

> You could not open a newspaper without the ads jumping out at you.
> [. . .] There were cons, miracle cures, ointments that heal everything
> for next to nothing, drugs that cocked a snook at medicine.[1]

Quacks were found mostly in the field of patent medicines. An enterprising person with a large sum of money to spend could launch such a product and make a fortune, even if the product in question cured nothing.[2]

A QUI DONNER LE GRAND PRIX DU SALON ?

RÉPONSE : Au spirituel artiste qui a exposé, salle 48, la Volupté élevant l'Amour au biberon, avec du Vin Mariani.

Color advertisement by Ferdinand Bac (1859–1952)
in *La Vie parisienne,*
May 6, 1905.

The Father
of Modern Advertising

This was Mariani's dilemma. Wishing to advertise his wine in order to expand his customer base, he decided on an innovative approach. He began by placing his first advertisement in *Le Figaro*, which had launched its cheap classified ads in 1869. From the beginning Mariani understood that successful advertising was cumulative and repetitive; if an ad did not appear regularly, potential buyers would lose interest. He then thought about other ways to advertise, looking for a more spectacular way to attract the public's attention besides just written ads. Potential customers had to be convinced that his wine was not just another "miracle cure," not just another product among the hundreds that filled the ad pages of the daily newspapers. He had to do better, because he knew he had an excellent product.

Since his competitors were accustomed to doing their own advertising for their products, Mariani wanted to find a way to have others promote his wine. It was a brilliant idea. Wouldn't impartial testimonials about the benefits of Vin Mariani be a thousand times more convincing than Mariani himself proclaiming the wonders of his wine? But how to get others to sing the praises of his product? The use of testimonials would become the key to marketing his coca wine to the world and would lead to one of the most amazing advertising campaign ever undertaken. The use of testimonials had existed in England since the beginning of the Victorian era; it was not uncommon to see high-profile individuals lending their names to a wide variety of products. But they did not do it for free. The *Edinburgh Review* discovered that, in 1843,

> Mr. Cockle's Anti-bilious Pills were recommended by, among others, ten dukes, five marquises, seventeen earls, eight viscounts, sixteen lords, one archbishop, fifteen bishops, the adjutant-general and the advocate-general. This list might give rise to curious speculations as to the comparative biliousness of the higher classes.[3]

The success enjoyed by Mariani in his testimonial-based campaign prompted other manufacturers to emulate this strategy, making it one of the most popular advertising techniques of the early twentieth century. In 1905 it was possible to buy unsolicited testimonials from an office in Washington, and an agency in Leeds was selling lists with the names of people suffering from various diseases. Any company could buy these lists and target their advertisements to those who might need their pills, syrups,

JUPITER ET CALISTO

Dessin de L. Vallet.

— Mais, mâtine, quel filtre lui fais-tu boire pour qu'il soit si épatant ?
— Ce que je viens de te faire boire à toi-même, un verre de VIN MARIANI.

Color advertisement by
Louis Vallet (1856–1940)
in *La Vie parisienne*,
November 5, 1905.

or lotions.[4] The use of testimonials by advertisers has never decreased. Nowadays a celebrity is used whenever a product needs to become better known or have its sales boosted, with the celebrity in question lending an image of exclusivity and authenticity. Mariani's use of testimonials as an advertising method is still cited today in the marketing bible that serves as a textbook for students of the subject worldwide.[5]

The Father
of Modern Advertising

Angelo Mariani would be the first, however, to get free testimonials from the most famous personalities. Mariani had the intuition that any person he approached would give a testimonial to him without asking anything in return. He realized that no one could remain indifferent to his request for a testimonial about his wine because the quality of the product was such that nobody would feel embarrassed to do so. It was a bold undertaking, but it proved successful: many celebrities were willing to give him their portrait accompanied by a handwritten appreciation of his wine, in response to receiving a few bottles or a case of the wine, the amount sent depending on the importance of the recipient. A journalist noted:

> How often has one heard this questioning exclamation about Angelo Mariani: But, how does he do it? [. . .] It must cost him a fortune! And how does he go about asking people who are sometimes in such high positions? Mariani could answer: It does not cost me anything . . . I do not ask or pay anything. Do as I do and it will be offered to you.[6]

Le Figaro tells how all this started:

> It was a spontaneous gesture from Gounod that would later lead to those testimonials expressing a gratitude made all the more sincere since the personal character of those expressing thanks excluded any suspicion of self-interest. As the composer of *Faust* complimented Mariani one day on the beneficial effects that coca had produced in him, Mariani replied, laughing: "You should tell me this in music!" The next day he received a hosanna in honor of the miraculous beverage. A few days later, Ambroise Thomas, Victorien Sardou, and Alexandre Dumas fils, who had been told about it, had fun sending Mariani some witty improvisations on the benefits of the famous wine. Mariani, with permission from the authors, published these attestations, thus inaugurating a method of advertising previously unknown and leading to a small revolution in the field of marketing. The idea was thought ingenious, as other spontaneous collaborations, no less illustrious, joined the first; all contemporary figures wanted to be included in the albums, which gave public recognition. So then Mariani the artist, forgetting the commercial considerations that led to his original endeavor, became attached—as his miraculous

Testimonial by Charles Gounod (1818–93).

collection increased—to presenting it in a form that made it valuable to bibliophiles and useful to historians. On this he spent a fortune.[7]

The *Albums Mariani*

Soon these testimonials were enough to form an anthology, a veritable collection of witty words. But one thing was missing: biographies of the contributors. This is where Mariani made his true masterstroke. He

Advertisement by Louis Vallet (1856–1940)
in *La Vie parisienne*, August 29, 1903.

Un jolie femme, un bon dîner, et un verre de vin MARIANI.....

decided to include the biographies of those who had sent him testimonials, thus creating a biographical directory of Belle Époque personalities. It was the first illustrated *Who's Who* ever published.

The great psychoanalyst Marie Bonaparte said in her memoirs that, in doing so, Mariani demonstrated great psychological shrewdness:

> But even more psychologically astute is how Mariani organized the publicity for his wine. A true genius of advertising, he imagined albums where all the celebrities of Paris and the provinces attest in statements, below their portraits, to the value of his magic elixir. [...] By thus combining the publicity for his wine with the vanity of others, the pharmacist Mariani has acquired a distinct position in the Parisian world.[8]

Color advertisement by
Louis Vallet (1856–1940)
in *La Vie parisienne,*
May 12, 1906.

The Father
of Modern Advertising

A first issue with twenty-four notices and portraits appeared in July 1891 under the title *Album Mariani*, followed by a second in 1892, and a third the following year. In 1894, all three were gathered into one volume entitled *Figures Contemporaines, Tirées de l'Album Mariani* ("Contemporary Figures, Drawn from the Mariani Albums"), the first in a series of fourteen such volumes that would be known to posterity under the name *Albums Mariani*. From 1892 to 1914, Mariani collected these testimonials and biographies in thirteen albums. His son Jacques published the fourteenth volume in 1925, a few years after Mariani's death.

Mariani, great bibliophile that he was, first had 500 copies printed on expensive paper with etched portraits, and with the volume offered to anyone who asked for it. But the requests became so numerous that Mariani decided to print a regular edition of several thousand copies on ordinary paper with woodcut portraits that sold at an affordable price.

Among the 1,086 portraits gathered in fourteen volumes, we can find three popes who honor him with a gold medal. According to Dr. Mortimer, for years Leo XIII, "had been supported in his ascetic retirement by a preparation of Mariani's Coca, of which a flask constantly worn is like the widow's cruse never empty."[9] There were also 16 sovereigns, 8 presidents, including 6 French presidents, 43 ministers, 37 field marshals and generals, 248 writers, 165 painters and sculptors, 30 composers, and 94 opera singers and actors (see a selection of Supplementary Testimonials at the end of the book).

American postcard with popes' medals given to Mariani.

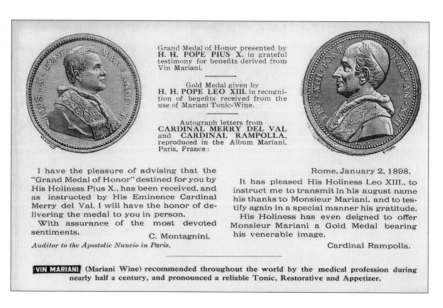

Grand Medal of Honor presented by H. H. POPE PIUS X. in grateful testimony for benefits derived from Vin Mariani.

Gold Medal given by H. H. POPE LEO XIII. in recognition of benefits received from the use of Mariani Tonic-Wine.

Autograph letters from CARDINAL MERRY DEL VAL and CARDINAL RAMPOLLA, reproduced in the Album Mariani, Paris, France:

I have the pleasure of advising that the "Grand Medal of Honor" destined for you by His Holiness Pius X., has been received, and as instructed by His Eminence Cardinal Merry del Val, I will have the honor of delivering the medal to you in person.

With assurance of the most devoted sentiments.

C. Montagnini.
Auditor to the Apostolic Nuncio in Paris.

Rome, January 2, 1898.

It has pleased His Holiness Leo XIII., to instruct me to transmit in his august name his thanks to Monsieur Mariani, and to testify again in a special manner his gratitude. His Holiness has even deigned to offer Monsieur Mariani a Gold Medal bearing his venerable image.

Cardinal Rampolla.

VIN MARIANI (Mariani Wine) recommended throughout the world by the medical profession during nearly half a century, and pronounced a reliable Tonic, Restorative and Appetizer.

A STATISTICAL DISTRIBUTION OF 905 TESTIMONIALS[10]

OCCUPATION	NUMBER REPRESENTED	STATISTICAL PERCENTAGE REPRESENTED
Painters, sculptors, composers, singers	283	31.3%
Writers	216	23.9%
Doctors	116	12.8%
Academies and institutes	88	9.72%
Ministries, diplomatic bodies	83	9.2%
Clergy (popes, cardinals, archbishops, bishops, abbots, monks)	40	4.4%
Miscellaneous	31	3.4%
Army (generals, colonels, lieutenant colonels, majors)	24	2.7%
Kings, queens, presidents	15	1.7%

The biographies were written by Mariani's secretary Joseph Uzanne (1850–1937), a witty society columnist of fin de siècle Paris. Each celebrity was entitled to a two-page spread on his or her life and work that included an engraved portrait with a signature in addition to their contribution to the glory of Vin Mariani: original prose or verse, a stave of music with lyrics, or a drawing or piece of sculpture.

Their publication was unanimously praised by critics, and the celebrity was such that—as a reporter for *Le Figaro* wrote—one day, the mayor of a small town in the south, warned about the presence of an imperial highness among the travelers on the Paris express, wished to welcome her in a way befitting her status. He wondered how he would recognize her. He consulted the stationmaster, who claimed to have the solution. He ran to his office and brought back the *Album Mariani*. He then had only to check the name and could recognize the person through her photograph. On another occasion a *Figaro* journalist witnessed a dispute between two young people. One of them was arguing that such and such a famous engraver had created a certain medal, while the other attributed it to a less famous colleague. To solve the problem, they agreed to consult reference books. The *Grand Larousse* encyclopedia was out of date. One of them then said: "I thought I saw a collection of *Albums Mariani* at the local library. That's what we need!" They went to the reading room of the library and flipped through the table of contents in the volumes to find the biography they needed. It did not take them long to find the answer,

The Father
of Modern Advertising

Color advertisement card for Biscuits Lu & Vin Mariani with image of the dancer Cléo de Mérode.

and the first announced to his friend that he was right: it was indeed Oscar Roty who had created the medal.[11]

Is it not surprising, asks the journalist,

To think that such a work originated in advertising? But what clever advertising, even philosophical, so to speak, is more ingeniously superior than the one that [. . .] claims both the virtues of a wine beneficial to men and the value of the men who attest to the excellence of this beverage!

He concluded that those who want to study advertising in this period and who would otherwise not have

> known and loved Mariani, for to know him is to love him, will find it difficult to understand the means by which this inventor and manufacturer of a powerful fortified wine could manage to gather around him so many illustrious men eager to serve his interests, without having to tie them to him by royal munificence. [...] This *altruistic and mutualistic* advertising that he introduced in his continuously published *Supplements* and *Albums* has been, as expected, imitated, copied, distorted, and caricatured by countless industrialists, because successful methods always invite plagiarists. However, no other than Mariani could have gathered around him so many famous people and celebrities giving instinctive sympathy to the attractive kindness of an incomparable man what they would certainly have refused to give to some ordinary concern or vulgar publicity.[12]

Many were those who enthusiastically welcomed the idea of Mariani publishing his "Gallery of Contemporaries," and they were not only men of letters and artists. Many personalities were concerned, and disapproved, above all, of the advertising methods used by most manufacturers. This is what the writer and bibliophile Octave Uzanne (1851–1931), brother of Joseph, had to say in his preface to the first *Album Mariani:*

> At a time when advertising is becoming brutally Americanized, when the millionaires of the industry seek, in the vulgarity of the advertisements, in the buffoonery of the poster art, any means of attracting attention, while the quacks with their chemical medications, condensed foods, quick fixes for aging, and all those who speculate on the masses and who live on advertising throw huge sums at the world to recommend their universal panaceas and impress the public mind surfeited from the sheer excess of the thing read, perceived, felt, and heard, it is comforting to see a gentleman in business who is artist enough, daring enough, and sure enough of his regard in the fields of literature, science, and the arts to channel these main resources

Sketch by Gustave Jossot (1866–1951) in *Supplément illustré*, 1905.

Dessin de *M. Jossot*, Artiste Peintre.

into a work as elevated, as useful, as complete in every respect as this great iconography, which, for posterity, will certainly be a precious reference.[13]

Presumably there was a form of competition in wit and talent among those who sent their testimonials. Or perhaps it was just a challenge, with poets, illustrators, and writers competing with each other to produce poems, drawings, and witticisms as successful as those of their colleagues. When Alexandre Dumas, fils was asked to compose a thought for his portrait, here is what he answered:

My dear, a thought, but it's harder to find than a comedy! [. . .] A scene is written in one morning, how many days does it take to find a thought of La Rochefoucauld? First, one should be La Rochefoucauld. But a thought for Mariani, a concise thought, deep, definitive, give me a year![14]

In 1898, a lawsuit became the topic of conversation. The famous photographer Leopold Reutlinger (1863–1937) took Mariani to the First Court of the Civil Tribunal of the Seine for reproducing in his *Albums* seventeen of his portraits of celebrities, among them Anatole France, Sarah Bernhardt, and Octave Mirbeau. Reutlinger asserted that the portraits were reproductions and forgeries of his own photographs and published without permission. Mariani argued that the photographer could not claim exclusive ownership of the portraits, and that he had obtained permission to publish the portraits from the persons in question. Several personalities, including Jules Massenet, Edouard Drumont, and José Maria de Heredia, took Mariani's side.

The court found on January 10, 1899, that Reutlinger had an unquestionable right to reproduction and forbade Mariani from future publication of the portraits in question. Mariani was sentenced to 500 francs in damages as well.[15] Beginning with *Album 10,* Mariani gave photographic credits for the illustrations.

In 1909, Mariani donated his personal collection of the first thirteen *Albums* to the Bibliothèque Nationale. The set, consisting of twenty-six volumes, is unique because it contains many original letters, watercolors, and drawings, some of which had never been published, or only fragments of which appeared in the published *Albums.* The volumes were sumptuously bound by the famous bookbinder Charles Meunier, "who has lavished on the panels and backs of these volumes small masterpieces of incised leather, inlays of medallions, harmonious mosaics, and watercolors signed by famous artists."[16] These bound books with inscriptions in gold leaf and a red coca flower on the back of each volume are tangible proof of the artistic taste of Mariani. Inserted between the pages are letters, invitations, drawings, advertisements and press clippings attesting to the importance of Mariani not only in France but also abroad. One finds an invitation to a party at the Elysée Palace from the president of the Republic, a six-page letter from Sarah Bernhardt, a drawing by Auguste Rodin, the death notice of Charles Gounod, a calligraphed letter from Emperor Don Pedro II of Brazil, and so forth.

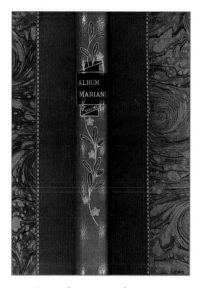

One of Mariani's fourteen leather-bound albums, where he published celebrity testimonials praising the excellence of his wine. Coca engravings comprise the motif.

Caricature by
Maurice Radiguet
(1866–1941) in
L'Assiette au beurre,
October 15, 1904.

In one of these letters, dated November 1902, the poet José Maria de Heredia, member of the French Academy, wrote the following to Mariani:

Today we entered the word *coca* in the Academy dictionary and I had the pleasure, thinking of you, to add to the old definition these [two]

The Father
of Modern Advertising

86

words: *coca wine.* I would have liked to include your name, but it is not customary. You would have had to be dead, and I prefer you to be alive.[17]

June 4, 1908, Dr. Jean Charcot, who was about to take the helm of the second French expedition to the South Pole, wrote to Mariani: "I am convinced that, like last time, your wine, your elixir, and your tea will render us the greatest service, and if we have any success, they will have been the key to it."

Returning from the expedition, Charcot wrote him again: "I can assure you that during our expedition we praised the Mariani wine and elixir. Many of us were seriously ill. Thanks to you, we were able to recover, and furthermore, when we were well, and in good health, we drank a glass of Vin Mariani, to your health!"[18]

> "I am convinced that Vin Mariani will contribute greatly toward the success of the French Antarctic expedition." —Dr. Jean-Baptiste Charcot, explorer; *Albums Mariani*, vol. 9

Themes of the *Albums*

EROTICISM

One can find in the *Albums* a number of testimonials about the erotic virtues of coca and Vin Mariani that were not selected for publication because they were considered too risqué. Among them is this little poem by the novelist Dubut de Laforest:

> *It happened that a vidame,*
> *Having taken advantage of a madam,*
> *Was found one morning*
> *Dry and emptied as a puppet,*
> *Ah, how sad he was*
> *To see his nature fall!*
> *But thanks to coca*
> *The cock has*
> *Shown up for the old man!*
> *That is how*
> *Our Angelo Mariani*
> *Raises what we think is done.*[19]

One of the main virtues attributed to Vin Mariani and highlighted in all the testimonials, is its efficacy as an aphrodisiac.

The Father of Modern Advertising

Postcard by
Francisque Desportes
(1849–1909).

Postcard by Maurice
Neumont (1868–1930).

Dr. Bonnaire, the chief obstetrician at Lariboisière Hospital, saw Vin Mariani as a cure for a decreasing population (*Albums,* vol. 8). The sculptor Ferdinand Gilbaut joined him in this view when he told of a maid, seeing her master feel sorry for not having children, who watered the garden cabbages with Vin Mariani (vol. 11). The advocate general at the Court of Cassation, G. Feuilloley, wanted to make its use mandatory in marriage (vol. 10). The hotshot lawyer Felix Decori said for his part that it was "the best antidote to divorce" (vol. 6).

French playwright Georges Feydeau told about a very beautiful woman who went one day to a famous old painter wishing that he would

Postcard by Jules Girardet (1856–1938).

Design for a bas-relief by Louis-Ernest Barrias (1841–1905) in *Albums Mariani*, vol. 7.

The Father of Modern Advertising

Postcard by
Félix Charpentier
(1858–1924)

Portrait
et sculpture bronze
cire perdue
de
M. *Félix Charpentier,*
Statuaire.

paint her in "'Venus Crowning Love.' So, to stimulate his numbed talent, he drank coca. This thing happened—how supernatural—the painter who had only Venus for model, when the session ended, had made Love" (vol. 5).

A number of testimonials used the homophony of the word *coca* with *cock* (Fr: *coq*), animal symbol of virility. The composer Ernest Reyer wished after drinking "six bottles of your admirable coca, the neighbor's wife would whisper in my ears. 'Oh Lord, what strength this old cock has!'" (vol. 4). Or the writer Catulle Mendes: "We have, thanks to coca wine—all the virtues that the cock has" (vol. 2). The cartoonist Henry Gerbault drew a character transformed into a cock after drinking Vin Mariani (vol. 9).

The drawings by some artists were very explicit. Jules Girardet showed a hunter drinking Vin Mariani with a comely maid, and has a caption that said: "After a glass of Mariani one can try to do two things at once . . ." (vol. 9).

Should we see a subconsciously deliberate mistake, a slip of the pen, in the terracotta design of Louis-Ernest Barrias's bas-relief that shows a naked woman caressing the neck of a bottle of Vin Mariani from which rays gush forth (vol. 7), or in the sculpture by Félix Charpentier showing a naked woman holding a bottle of Vin Mariani between her thighs, her right hand covering her pubis, trying to uncork the bottle? The caption adds to the ambiguity: "You think I bust a gut pulling the cork? No! Since I take Vin Mariani, it comes all by itself" (vol. 12).

War

After Eros comes Thanatos. The army indeed found Vin Mariani to its taste and deemed it useful and effective. The joint staff chief of the army, General Boisdeffre, wished, "that every soldier in the French army would have a bottle of Vin Mariani in his bag on the day of the battle" (vol. 6). The commander of the expeditionary force in China, General Pélacot, believed: "If I had known about Vin Mariani in 1900, the siege of Tientsin would have seemed much less difficult to me. In the future, I will not embark on a colonial expedition without a case of Vin Mariani, this first-rate fortifying tonic" (vol. 12). General Gallieni, for his part, related an episode in the Tonkin War, where the distribution of cases of Vin Mariani to the exhausted soldiers allowed them to brilliantly storm a den of pirates, despite the latter's vigorous resistance (vol. 7).

"In order to keep the monopoly on decisiveness and energy in France, the export of Vin Mariani should be prohibited."
—Marshal Franchet d'Esperey; *Supplément illustré*, 1922

The makers of Le suprême coca use a symbol often seen in Mariani's advertisements, the rooster, in this advertisement card.

The Father of Modern Advertising

Vignette from
Albums Mariani, vol. 13.

Field Marshal Joffre as well thanked Mariani for the "bottles of his wine generously sent to general headquarters during the war" (*Supplément illustré*, 1927).

Field Marshal Franchet d'Esperey was an advocate of extreme measures: "In order to keep the monopoly on decisiveness and energy in France, the export of Vin Mariani should be prohibited" (vol. 14). General Weygand, for his part, did not mince words: "No more neurotics, no more layabouts! But vigorous and ardent Frenchmen at their jobs thanks to Vin Mariani" (*Supplément illustré*, 1923). Vin Mariani would receive the highest blessing from Field Marshal Pétain: "The French had to win the war, since they had on their side Coca Mariani, the king of wines" (vol. 14).

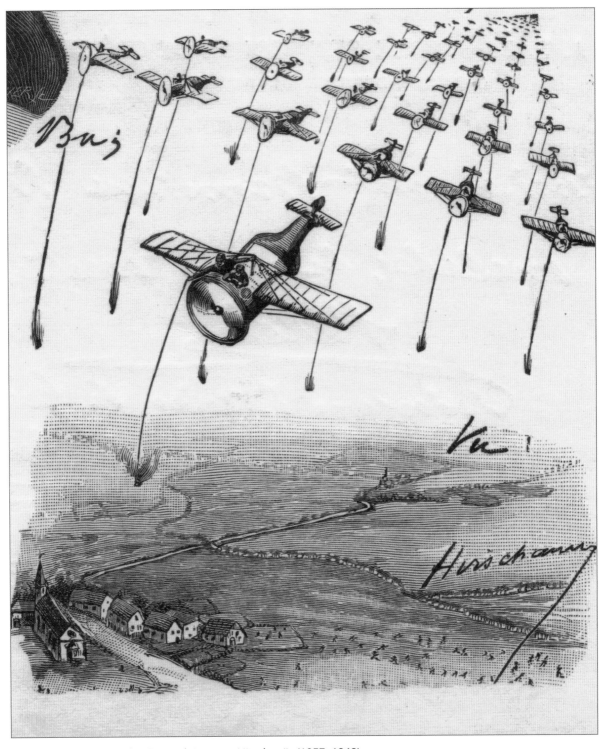

Drawing by General Auguste Hirschauër (1857–1943)
in *Supplément illustré*, 1913.

THE ELIXIR OF LIFE

Another virtue of Vin Mariani put forward in the various testimonials was its efficacy in conserving or even prolonging life, as would an elixir of life or a fountain of youth. Many were testimonials of old men such as this one from Nadar: "Without your elixir of life, my good Mariani, perhaps I wouldn't have been able to thank you for my seventy-six years" (vol. 4). The painter Louis Gratia was ninety-five when he paid "tribute to Mr. Mariani, and his wonderful wine," and signed as "an old grateful Faust" (vol. 12). The dean of them all was undoubtedly

Postcard by Albert Laurens (1870–1934).

The Father of Modern Advertising

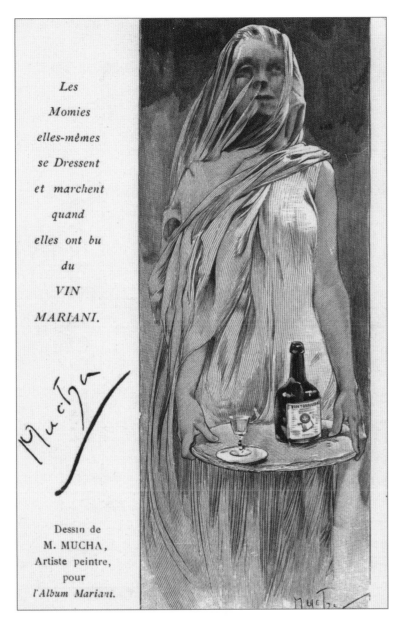

Les
Momies
elles-mêmes
se Dressent
et marchent
quand
elles ont bu
du
VIN
MARIANI.

Dessin de
M. MUCHA,
Artiste peintre,
pour
l'Album Mariani.

"Mummies themselves would
get up and walk if they but
drank Vin Mariani!"
—Alphonse Mucha, painter;
Albums Mariani, vol. 4

Postcard by
Alphonse Mucha
(1860–1939).

François Fertiault, of the Society of Men of Letters: At ninety-nine, he was confident that, thanks to Vin Mariani, he would celebrate his centenary (vol. 13). Jules Verne noted that, "Since a single bottle of the extraordinary Vin Mariani is enough to ensure you a hundred years of existence, I'll be alive until 2700! Well, I have no objection!" (vol. 3). Leonce Bénédite, curator (*conservateur*) at the Musée du Luxembourg, noted that Vin Mariani "conserves better than I do, it is the supreme Conservative" (vol. 12).

The Father
of Modern Advertising

Mucha went even further, since "Mummies themselves would get up and walk if they but drank Vin Mariani!" (vol. 4).

It even rejuvenated one, if we can believe Tristan Bernard: "Effect of Vin Mariani: I am thirty-eight years younger, and I just started to write" (vol. 13).

Finally, we are informed by Jules Romains that it was such an effective miracle cure that "Dr. Knock strictly prohibits the use of Vin Mariani among his patients because he had seen a worrying drop in the number of his consultations and treatments" (*Supplément illustré* 1932).

POLITICS

Even in politics, Vin Mariani played a role. Several presidents (or future presidents) of the French Republic recommended its use. Among them, Albert Lebrun, who believed, "Politicians should be at the forefront of those who sing the praises of Vin Mariani. No profession requires tonic and comforting more than theirs" (*Supplément illustré* 1932). Emile Loubet just offered a sober "Homage to Mr. Mariani, the popularizer of coca" (vol. 12). Gaston Doumergue, meanwhile, admitted consuming it: "It pleases the taste; it does one good. That's why I am loyal to Vin Mariani" (vol. 14).

For the prime minister Edouard Herriot: "Vin Mariani gives us the courage to carry out our task" (vol. 14). To the minister of the interior Louis Barthou, Vin Mariani was a guarantee of a long political life: "To the potential successors who wonder and worry about the longevity of the Meline government I reveal the secret [...] for long-time employment: all its members drink Vin Mariani" (vol. 4).

The colonial secretary Raphael Millies-Lacroix believed that Vin Mariani: "is precious to the old men of the Parliament; it warms their brains and hearts and kindles their noble inspirations in preparing laws for the Republic" (vol. 11). The member of Parliament and publicist Jules Delafosse opined, however, that it was "not wise to recommend it to the members of Parliament. It might encourage them to undertake too much, and their behavior never seems to me so commendable than when they do nothing!" (vol. 12).

This was confirmed, in his own way, by another president of the Republic, Paul Deschanel: "Allow any quantity of Coca Mariani for the president, but not too much for members of Parliament" (vol. 5). The journalist and politician Henri Rochefort thought the government itself

"Your precious wine has completely reformed my constitution. You should certainly offer some to the French government." —Henri Rochefort, politician; *Albums Mariani*, vol. 2

needed Vin Mariani when he wrote: "Dear Mr. Mariani: Your precious wine has completely reformed my constitution. You should certainly offer some to the French government" (vol. 2). The publicist and politician Henry de Jouvenel was more pessimistic: "There is much talk about rejuvenating the Constitution. The only statesman who has succeeded at it so far is called Mariani" (vol. 14).

SPORTS

Vin Mariani also enabled the accomplishment of physical feats in sports. The car manufacturer Count Dion noted, "When, in the case of a big rush, in the day before a race, for example, we are forced to ask our mechanics to work the night shift, we kindle their zeal and support their prowess with general and repeated distributions of Vin Mariani" (vol. 5).

Or there is this from the great tennis champion Suzanne Lenglen: "At the slightest lapse . . . quick! A glass of Vin Mariani!" (*Supplément illustré,* 1926).

The ultimate endorsement, from the founder of the modern Olympic Games, Baron Pierre de Coubertin, is this: "Vin Mariani was allowed for athletes who were training for the Olympic Games; at the end of the competitions, the winners used to offer a basket of it to Olympian Jupiter as a token of gratitude" (*Supplément illustré* 1929).

ALCOHOLISM

In a curious paradox—if one believes some of the testimonials—Vin Mariani could even help combat alcoholism!

"The dangers of alcoholism could be averted, if each one of us would ask only the bountiful Vin Mariani for the physical relief and the peak energy necessary to do great works," said the director of the general administration of public hospitals, Gustave Mesureur (vol. 9). The president of the Chamber of Deputies, Paul Painlevé, was not afraid to declare "war against alcoholism, but honor to Vin Mariani" (vol. 14). The father of the BCG vaccine and student of Pasteur, Albert Calmette, did not hesitate to declare: "Absinthe kills the man, Mariani's coca wine kills absinthe" (vol. 11).

In any case, according to the painter Jules Grün: "Mariani! Superior to the best wines, does not give even the slightest hangover" (vol. 9). And the member of the Academy of Medicine and director of the National Institute of Agronomy, Paul Regnard, could dream: "Ah!

"The Michelin tire 'drinks the obstacle' but gets flat! I drink Vin Mariani . . . and I rise again!" —The Michelin brothers, tire engineers; *Supplément illustré,* 1907

Postcard by Sem
(1863–1934)

The Father
of Modern Advertising

Dessin de M. GRUN,
Artiste peintre,
pour *l'Album Mariani*.

if only in the 550,000 cafés in France, we only drank Vin Mariani"
(vol. 11).

THE VOICE

A number of testimonials also highlighted the benefits of Vin Mariani
for the voice, whether in the case of singing or speechmaking. Among the
ones worth quoting is the great *chanteuse réaliste* (realist singer) Yvette
Guilbert, for whom there is no doubt that "If I had not often drunk Vin
Mariani, my poor vocal cords would have suffered considerably from
the strain of all my travels, but Mariani saved me. Therefore, I am very
grateful to him!" (vol. 3). For Sarah Bernhardt: "Mariani coca wine is a
precious friend for my throat" (vol. 5). Another great actress of the twentieth century, Madeleine Renaud, wanted to make use of Vin Mariani
mandatory at the Comédie Française: "Candidates . . . for membership
should drink only Vin Mariani" (*Supplément illustré,* 1928). For the
movie actress Gaby Morlay "Vin Mariani is a tonic that is never used in
vain" (*Supplément illustré,* 1927).

The great singer Emma Calvé testified: "I followed your advice to
fight my cold. I took hot grog with your delicious coca wine and I could
sing *Carmen* last night. With my warmest thanks." (vol. 2).

The preacher at Notre-Dame, Father Monsabré, confirmed: "This

On a dit : « Le Vin de **Mariani** donne de la voix, » et moi j'ajoute : « Il fortifie les opinions et la santé. »

André **Brouillet,**
en hommage au **Vin Mariani.**

Postcard by André Brouillet (1857–1914).

"Vin Mariani is a tonic that is never used in vain."
—Gaby Morlay, actress; *Supplément illustré,* 1927

excellent coca wine. It provides what the cock has: a loud voice" (vol. 2). For the abbot Gayraud, member of Parliament from Brittany: "Among my oratorical precautions I include a small glass of Vin Mariani. It's the 'one for the road' in the speaking profession" (vol. 4). The lawyer and future minister of justice, César Campinchi, estimated that, to him, "in the pointed battles in criminal court, one glass of Mariani is an argument. Two glasses is the acquittal!" (*Supplément illustré* 1927).

One last testimonial, but certainly not the least, emanated from His Royal Highness, Ferdinand I of Bulgaria: "After twenty or more audiences during the morning; then receiving the diplomatic corps; presiding over the council of ministers for several hours; and still to give a political speech before hundreds of the representatives of the nation, more or less anxious to detect any weakness in rhetoric in the head of state: quickly, one or two glasses of this excellent Vin Mariani. . . . All hesitation disappears, and words flow clearly, easily, and convincingly." (vol. 9)[20]

The Father
of Modern Advertising

The *Suppléments illustrés*

Mariani also wanted to disseminate these testimonials to the general public. The best way, the easiest way, was to use the newspapers. He met with the director of *Le Figaro* to ask him about the possibility of inserting some additional pages devoted to these portraits. A pilot edition of four pages including fifty-five portraits was published February 12, 1893, in the newspaper. Instead of prints, celebrity portraits were replaced by photographs and autographs, but without the biographical text. The first insertion was such a success that the continuation of the *Suppléments illustrés* was assured for years to come. The second issue appeared December 5, 1895, and contained forty-two portraits. The series continued in years following in nearly a dozen newspapers: *Le Journal, L'Eclair, Le Monde illustré, Le Matin, Le Temps,* and so on, and would soon expand to sixteen pages. In all, twenty-nine series would follow, the last appearing in 1932. After the war, the total number of pages was reduced to eight.

It should be noted that some of the testimonials that were published in the *Suppléments* were not included in the *Albums;* there are even new testimonials in the *Suppléments* from people already included in the *Albums.* In total, 1,834 testimonials and drawings were published in these *Suppléments,* therefore more than 700 were never published in the *Albums.*

According to Joseph Uzanne, 800,000 copies of these *Suppléments* were printed in 1907 alone.[21]

Cover of
the *Supplément illustré,*
1932

Patronage:
The Tales, the Postcards, and the Medals

Alongside the *Albums Mariani,* the "father of coca" had the idea of making his products known through other means and other media: books, postcards, posters, menus, blotters, and medals made by famous artists of the time, including Oscar Roty (1846–1911), to whom we owe several silver coca-themed objects: matchboxes, dance cards, pill boxes, cufflinks, tie pins, sealing stamps, and bottle and glass holders.

Mariani also loved literature and was a bibliophile with a large collection of books. In 1888, he had an idea to publish a book of stories devoted to coca. The result was a collection of thirteen tales written by popular authors: among them, Armand Silvestre, Paul Arène, Jules Claretie, Octave Uzanne, Fréderic Mistral, and Albert Robida.

Watercolor by Albert Robida (1848–1926).
Courtesy of E. Mariani.

The Father
of Modern Advertising

Coca-themed silver objects made for Mariani by Oscar Roty (1846–1911): dance card, tie pin, and pill box. Courtesy of F. Arzeno.

Original drawing by Enrique Atalaya (1851–1913) on Angelo Mariani's own copy of the tale *La plante enchantée* (The enchanted plant) by Armand Silvestre, 1895. Courtesy of E. Mariani.

Illustration by Louis Morin (1855–1938) from the coca tale *Trois filles et trois garçons* (Three Girls and Three Boys), 1899.

ENVOI

*Mariani! Mon financier
N'étant ni de roc, ni d'acier,
Mais de fragile chair humaine,
Fût mort, vivement, à son tour,
Devant sa trinité d'amour, —
Car trop de joie est grande peine; —
Mais, comme il se croyait fini,
Il but ton vin, Mariani!
Et, sur-le-champ, reprit... haleine!*

These stories were in print until 1904 under the name *Contes de la collection Angelo Mariani* (Tales from the Collection of Angelo Mariani). The print runs were between 300 and 500 copies, and they were published in a deluxe edition in quarto format, including a small number on Japanese paper, and illustrated mostly in color, though some titles in the popular smaller-edition format had illustrations in black and white. Albert Robida (1848–1926) illustrated more than half of the tales. Below are the plots of some of the stories:

Original drawing by Enrique Atalaya (1851–1913) on Angelo Mariani's own copy of the tale *La plante enchantée* (The enchanted plant) by Armand Silvestre, 1895. Courtesy of E. Mariani.

- The first of these tales, *Le Cas du vidame* (The case of the vidame), by Louis de Beaumont and illustrated by Robida, appeared in 1888, and tells of the tribulations of the old Vidame de Grand Chastré, husband of the young and beautiful Thibaulde, whom he fails to honor properly both on the wedding night and later. Faced with his mother-in-law's reproaches and sarcasm from his neighbors he decides to consult doctors, magicians, and astrologers, begging them to help him. In desperation, one of the doctors recommends that he call "an illustrious apothecary named Mariani, who has a pharmacy in Paris very well known for his marital therapy."[22] His secret: coca. After three bottles of the precious elixir, the vidame was finally able to satisfy his wife, who soon bears him triplets.

- In *Explication* (1894), by Jules Claretie and illustrated by Robida, the author recounts the exploits of Hercules, who, thanks to the powerful effects of Vin Mariani, discovered America before Columbus.

- In *La plante enchantée* (The enchanted plant) (1895), by Armand Silvestre and illustrated by Robida, the mother and the lover of the beautiful Izoline decide to marry her to the rich old Baron des Engrumelles in the hope that she would soon become a rich widow. But a Spanish friend of the baron, back from the Americas, introduces him to a wonderful plant that gives him the strength and ability to beget a child. His chaplain makes a soothing wine with the plant, the secret of which was to be revealed only to a man with "sea-green eyes and a beautiful white beard"—the Reverend Brother Angelo Mariani.

- In *Les secrets des Bestes* (The secrets of the beasts) (1896), by Frédéric Mistral and illustrated by Robida, the author discovers in a library in Carpentras (Provence), a sixteenth-century manuscript that tells

Illustration by Albert Robida (1848–1926) from the coca tale *Le secret de Polichinelle* (Punchinello's secret), 1897.

The Father of Modern Advertising

Cover illustration by Léon Lebègue (1863–1944) from the coca tale *Pervenche* (Periwinkle), 1900.

of a woodcutter who overhears three secrets while listening to a conversation among three wild beasts. The first two secrets allow him to get one hundred thousand *reales* from the king of Spain and to be appointed a Spanish grandee. The third concerns coca, which allows him to heal the princess and marry her.

🌿 In *Un chapitre inédit de Don Quichotte* (An unpublished chapter from Don Quixote) (1898), by Jules Claretie and illustrated by José Atalaya, we see Sancho Panza restore vigor to his master and prolong his life thanks to the gourd of precious elixir that Don Pacheco gave him. After the death of his master, Sancho finds Pacheco: "Back from the West Indies with a boatload of green leaves, gray-green, soft, elastic, and plump, from a shrub [. . .] that Pizarro had once seen rolled between the fingers of the Inca; it was with the leaves of this tree of life that the tax was paid, in part, by the Indians to the victorious Spaniards and to the canons of the cathedral of Cuzco, without counting the bishop, who collected their annual incomes as fat as the belly of Sancho himself."[23]

🌿 *La panacée du capitaine Hauteroche* (The panacea of Captain Hauteroche) (1899), by Octave Uzanne and illustrated by Eugene

Illustration by Léon Lebègue from the coca tale *Pervenche* (Periwinkle), 1900.

The Father of Modern Advertising

Courboin, offers the recollections of an old soldier who survived the Chouans war, including the campaign in Saxony and the retreat from Russia, thanks to coca wine. Since then, Angelo Mariani makes him famous throughout France: "Corsican conqueror and campaigner," his name deserves to be associated with that of Napoleon.

- *Pervenche* (Periwinkle) (1900), by Maurice Bouchor and illustrated by Leon Lebègue, is the story of a young girl saved by her fiancé, Robert, from the clutches of William, lord of Freneuse-of-the-Turnips, by passing a physical test thanks to a magic drink from the dwarf Angelo Mariani. This drink will allow the young couple to have twelve children in the four years following their marriage!

- In *Le château de la grippe* (Influenza castle) (1904), by Albert Robida and illustrated by his daughter Emilie, the inhabitants of Anémicmacville-sur-Seine are struck by a terrible epidemic of influenza, a microbe battalion led by the marshal Grippetoukru. The young Zezette, the only one spared, accidentally discovers a small chapel with a statue, in front of which she prays. Along

Illustration by Emilie Robida (1881–1981) from the coca tale *Le château de la grippe* (Influenza castle), 1904.

Illustration by Emilie Robida (1881–1981) from the coca tale *Le château de la grippe* (Influenza castle), 1904.

The Father of Modern Advertising

Illustration by Emilie Robida in
Le château de la grippe (Influenza castle), 1904.

comes a hermit who informs her that she is praying to Saint Coca, an American saint. He takes her to visit his little hermitage, full of retorts and stills. Touched by her distress, he pours from the retorts and stills hordes of gnomes shaped like bottles that go through the city destroying the microbes, while the rooster in the belfry shouts "Cocaricoca" ("cock-a-doodle-do" in Peruvian). The city regains health and joie de vivre, while the good hermit flies away in his chariot holding in his arms "A huge bottle [. . .] on the label one can read 'Mariani Coca Wine,' and all around squads of flasks, decorated with the same triumphant label, trotted, swarmed, and crowded in countless rows to the sound of cheers."

The Father
of Modern Advertising

Illustration by Emilie Robida (1881–1981) from the coca tale
Le château de la grippe (Influenza castle), 1904.

Mariani also published a play titled *La fleur de coca* (1892) that was put on "for the first and only time in Angelo Mariani's Theatre June 29, 1892." Paul Arène's text with twelve full-page glyptographs described the love of Pierrot and Columbine. The setting is "a site at once ideal and Peruvian." Among other things, we see Columbine pouring Pierrot some

Postcard of schoolchildren drinking Vin Mariani.

Vin Mariani: "This living gold, this fluid gold, which makes an exhausted stallion a thoroughbred!"[24]

In 1900 Mariani also published a first series of 60 postcards with the drawing on the left side of the card. Some were republished, with the drawing occupying the entire card, between 1909 and 1912 for the publication of a set of 150 postcards. These were mailed in five packets of 30 cards each, selling for the low price of ten cents. A number of these cards were published especially for the American market.

The cards reproduced the drawings for and about Vin Mariani that were published in the *Albums*. They were signed by major artists, including Eugène Grasset, Mucha, Cappiello, Steinlen, Chéret, Robida, Auguste Lepère, Eugène Carrière, Henri Le Sidaner, and Lucien Levy-Dhurmer. The themes were many—social, historical, hygienic, comic,

Postcard by Emile-André
Boisseau (1842–1923)

Portrait of Mariani on a bronze medal, 1910,
by Louis Patriarche (1872–1955).

and so on. Among other things, there are portraits of aviators singing the praises of Vin Mariani along with schoolchildren and even babies drinking the precious nectar.[25]

A dozen medals and plaques, single- and double-sided, in gold, silver,

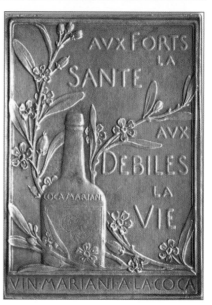

Top to bottom, from left to right: bronze medal on coca and Vin Mariani, 1906, by Louis-Eugène Mouchon (1843–1914); silver medal, 1908, by Victor Peter (1840–1918); bronze medal, 1908, by Louis Patriarche (1872–1955); silver medal, 1906, by Louis-Eugène Mouchon (1843–1914); silver medal, 1895, by Oscar Roty (1846–1911).

and bronze, and with Vin Mariani and coca as their subject, were engraved by a half dozen renowned medalists, including Oscar Roty and Eugène Mouchon (1843–1911).[26]

The father of the modern poster, Jules Chéret (1836–1932), also designed a poster for Vin Mariani in 1894, with a slightly different version for the U.S. market.

All of these advertising achievements of Mariani's are today highly prized by collectors and fetch significant prices. For pleasure, and at his own expense, Mariani also published a few books for collectors in editions of one hundred copies, illustrated by Albert Robida.[27]

In 1892, Mariani discreetly supported the creation of a magazine called *Simple Revue,* which lasted until 1924, and attracted young talent. It was a bimonthly whose editor, George Régnal, wanted to reach an audience attuned to cultural and social themes. Mariani's doings, travels, and dinners were often mentioned in the section called "The Arts and the World."

6 The Host of All Hosts

From the Restaurant Ledoyen
to the Villa at Valescure

Photography of Mariani at the opening of the *Salon des artistes français* (Exhibition of French Artists), 1905.

Mariani's conviviality was legendary and attracted people to him. Dinners he regularly gave at his home in rue Scribe were famous for the quality of the food served. According to a participant:

> If there is a house where the reception is exquisite, it is that of Mr. Angelo Mariani. [...] He frequently likes to gather around him a bright and genuinely affectionate elite.[1]

Every year beginning in 1898 he hosted a lunch at the famous restaurant Ledoyen for the opening of the *Salon des artistes français* (Exhibition of French Artists): "The meeting was very gay. It was decided to repeat it the following year at the same place, at Ledoyen. The following year, we were thirty. And it was even more joyful. The opening-day luncheon was established."

There were 10 guests at the first lunch, and then 110 in 1913, the last lunch that Mariani gave. Among the guests were many celebrities of the era: General Gallieni, Prince Roland Bonaparte, Jules Claretie, Jean Richepin, Albert Robida, Albert Sarraut, and Gaston Calmette. A witness at these banquets, a reporter from *Le Figaro,* recalled

> This generous man was the most modest of men. He took his place some distance from the head table. [...] He did not speak at all, but

Menu drawn by Albert Robida (1848–1926) for the lunch at restaurant Ledoyen, 1912.

simply, at the end of the meal, glided from table to table to offer wonderful cigars (made expressly for him in Havana) to his guests, whom he thanked for accepting them.

Meanwhile young girls passed by with a piggy bank designed by Oscar Roty to claim from each person attending the price of the meal: 25 cents.

The Host
of All Hosts

Menu drawn by Albert Robida (1848–1926) for the lunch at restaurant Ledoyen, 1905.

It was a price fixed once and for all, and no one escaped from paying. Mariani considered it his duty and joy to give alms as a natural accompaniment to a good meal. So it was usual, at his table, to ask any guest, whoever he was, for nickels. These nickels were put into a piggy bank and delivered, when the piggy bank was full, to the fund for the Orphelinat des Arts, a foster home for the arts.[2]

Postcard of the Orphelinat des Arts (Arts Orphanage).

The Orphelinat des Arts association, which Mariani took care of, was recognized in 1882 as a public service organization. It was founded in 1880 by the actress Marie Laurent, and helped by friends such as Sarah Bernhardt, as an education center for young girls who were the children of dramatic artists, painters, sculptors, architects, writers, musicians, journalists, and literary people. In 1887, the association benefitted from its first legacy, from Gustave Doré, which allowed it to buy a house in Courbevoie (near Paris), which is still active today. The house accommodated eighty

Photograph of Mariani and friends at an outdoor luncheon. Courtesy of Association des amis d'Albert Robida.

Menu drawn by Albert Robida (1848–1926) for the lunch at the restaurant Ledoyen, 1909.

residents then. In 1893, Oscar Roty had the idea of creating an equivalent association for boys, which was called the Fraternité artistique (Artists Brotherhood). Mariani was vice president from 1911 to 1914. The two associations merged in 1912.[3]

On the occasion of the dinners at his home in rue Scribe or the lunches at Ledoyen, Mariani had illustrated menus made that were given to the guests. Most were designed and drawn by the famous illustrator and visionary novelist Albert Robida, running from 1891 to 1901 for the dinners in rue Scribe and from 1903 to 1913 for the lunches at Ledoyen. In the upper part of each is a humorous drawing depicting the preparation of a fancy meal or a joyful meeting with guests from different periods of history.

For the luncheons at Ledoyen, the menus are more satirical, such as the ones where visitors must swallow the contents of paint cans with a brush, the size and extravagance of the hats of the women are mocked, or a charge is levied against the institute or the various avant-gardes. The lower part of the menu was reserved for the descriptions of the various dishes.[4]

A famous 1911 painting by Jules-Alexandre Grün (1868–1938), *Un*

Un vendredi au Salon des artistes français (Friday at the Exhibition of French Artists) 1911, painting by Jules-Alexandre Grün (1868–1938). Copyright C. Lancien, C. Loisel/ R. M. M. Rouen Normandie. Courtesy of the Musée des Beaux-Arts de Rouen.

Vendredi au Salon des Artistes français (Friday at the Exhibition of French Artists), with its imposing dimensions—twenty by ten feet—and with nearly a hundred characters, beautifully captures the atmosphere of, and is important testimony about, Parisian society during la Belle Époque. The whole of Paris is shown here, from the painter Harpignies in conversation with the secretary of state for fine arts Dujardin-Beaumetz, the prefect Lépine with Yvette Guilbert, and Gabriel Fauré with the painters Luc-Olivier Merson, Fernand Cormon, Georges Rochegrosse, Léon Bonnat, Édouard Detaille, and Grün himself. In the foreground—Angelo Mariani.

The Host
of All Hosts

Once a year, he also gave a costume party for all his friends. At one of these balls a participant arrived disguised as a coca leaf![5]

In summer, Mariani spent his holidays at his home in the South of France at Valescure, near Saint-Raphaël, a village where several of his friends had also bought properties. Among them was the medalist Oscar Roty, who had moved to Villa Marie, where he had a workshop and where he executed many of his works, such as the famous *La Semeuse* (The Sower):

> Is it not in Valescure, in the beautiful estate of Lord Amherst, that you can pick a branch from the olive tree that provided the model for the image on the back of our French coin, *La Semeuse*? It was in September 1896. . . . Through the care of Mr. Angelo Mariani a commemorative silver plaque was fastened to the legendary tree. . . . We hope that it lives to be more than a hundred years old, and thus becomes one of the curiosities of the area.[6]

SAINT-RAPHAEL VALESCURE — *Les petits Eclaireurs Raphaëlois à la Villa Andréa*

Postcard of Mariani with young scouts
in his garden in Valescure.

Villa Marie was occupied during the summer of 1924 by F. Scott Fitzgerald, who wrote *The Great Gatsby* there. It was, he writes:

> A clean cool villa set in a large garden on a hill above town. It was what we had been looking for all along. There was a summerhouse and a sand pile and two bathrooms and roses for breakfast and a gardener who called me milord.[7]

Photo of Villa Andréa.

Mariani built a villa in 1889 on the ten hectares of land that he had just bought. Made of marble, the villa combined Moorish and classical styles, and Mariani named it Andréa in honor of his daughter, Andrée, who had died at the age of nineteen.

It was accessed from rue Théodore Rivière, named after the sculptor, and the first thing one saw, mounted on the gate, was a bronze plaque called *The Nymph* that Roty had engraved to honor coca; closer to the door to the vestibule there was another plaque, *In labore quies*. Three other large plaques were attached to the walls and signed by either Eugène Mouchon or Pierre Lenoir. In the garden there were two sculptures by Théodore Rivière (1857–1912): *The djinn ou le lanceur de pierre* (The Djinn, or Stone Thrower) and a half-ton block of bronze depicting *Attila et les hordes de Huns* (Attila and the Hordes of Huns).

Autochrome Lumière of Mariani at his house in Valescure. Courtesy of E. Mariani.

Postcard of Mariani in front
of the fountain at Valescure.

At the foot of the stairs was a large polychrome earthenware piece eight feet by six, inlaid in the wall and depicting the *Les Cambodgiennes du monument de Sisowath* (The Cambodians from the Monument of Sisowath), by the same Rivière.

The garden was filled with lush tropical trees such as palms, fig, banana, cactus, pepper, and persimmon, as well as with exotic flowers like camellia, hibiscus, and datura.

This luxuriance was not only because of the climate but also a small stream, La Siagnole, that ran through the property. Mariani built a fountain that had a bronze nymph by Théodore Rivière stretched out over a rock and holding a cup to the fountainhead just outside his property. The sculpture was unfortunately melted down during World War II.[8] The inauguration of the fountain took place February 27, 1905, with the mayor of Saint-Raphaël in attendance. According to a witness:

This exquisite work is the result of funds from the games of crapette (double solitaire) at Villa Andréa. A plaque preserves the names of

Photo of Mariani with a friend in front of his house.

these gambling friends: Rivière, Roty, Xavier Paoli, Mariani, and the doctors Lutaud and Labbé.

Many friends came to stay at Villa Andréa:

To name all those who came here would include a quarter of the famous personalities from the *Album Mariani*. [. . .] Many come back every year at different seasons, with the fidelity of migratory birds.[9]

The Host
of All Hosts

Photo of Mariani with friends in front of his house.

Among the visitors, we can mention the writers and poets Edmond Rostand, Jules Verne, Alphonse Daudet, Pierre Loti, Courteline, Paul Verlaine, Frédéric Mistral, José Maria de Heredia, as well the Lumière brothers and Sarah Bernhardt.[10]

The great psychoanalyst Marie Bonaparte, then very young, was invited to Villa Andréa and describes Mariani in her memoirs: "He is an elderly, round and jovial man, with a red face, pleasing, beaming, and surrounded by a large white beard. He looks at me with his good grandfatherly eyes."[11]

Villa Andréa was unfortunately demolished a century later, in 1990.[12]

7 The Time of Ordeals: The Imitators

From Vin des Incas to Coca-Cola

In France

Mariani would soon be confronted with a number of major problems in relation to his business. His success made others envious and very quickly prompted a host of imitators who began to market similar preparations. Although the popularity of coca would become huge, none of these other preparations would be as successful as Vin Mariani, because they were often said to be of inferior quality.

As Émile Gautier noted in *Le Figaro:*

> Indeed, he was not lacking for rivals, and even enemies. Is it not the eternal law? But in the face of growing success they soon had to retreat and admit defeat. [. . .] Counterfeiters—and they too, were legion—could not have been happier. They imagined that they had a good game in making a liqueur endowed with the most wonderful virtues, but in their myopic view thought all they had to do was take a more or less authentic drinkable wine with some coca added and put it in reach of anyone. [. . .] Counterfeiters got nothing for their trouble.[1]

In the last decade of the nineteenth century, dozens of French pharmacists began to sell and advertise tonic coca wine, either pure or mixed

Coca des Incas poster, ca. 1899, anonymous. Courtesy of J. Santo Domingo.

with other tonic plants such as cinchona or kola nut. In 1881, a journalist from *The Therapeutic Gazette* found that in Paris,

> A number of chemists make a specialty of coca, and all, without exception, prepare coca wine on the prescription of a physician. One finds coca leaves for sale at all drug-shops in Paris.[2]

In the years 1880 to 1920 one could find nearly one hundred different coca wines or elixirs, often mixed with the other two tonics in vogue that

Coca des Incas poster, 1896, by Charles Lévy (1850–1900). Courtesy of J. Santo Domingo.

were made from kola nuts and cinchona bark (quinine).[3] Among these we can mention:

- *Coca des Incas,* created in the 1880s, and for which four posters are known: two by anonymous artists, one in 1895 and another circa 1899; one circa 1900 from the workshop of Hugo d'Alesi (1849–1906); and the fourth in 1896 by Charles Lévy (1850–1900).
- *Vin des Incas,* which contained coca and glycerophosphate of lime,

The Time of Ordeals:
The Imitators

Posters of *Coca des Incas*. Courtesy of J. Santo Domingo.
Left: 1895, anonymous, and right: ca. 1900 by Hugo d'Alesi (1849–1906).

Vin des Incas poster, 1899, by Alphonse Mucha (1860–1939). Courtesy of J. Santo Domingo.

became famous thanks to the poster drawn in 1899 by Alphonse Mucha (1860–1939).

- *Lox,* "a tonic-aperitif par excellence based on kina-loxa, coca, and kola." A poster for it was made in 1895 by Georges Meunier (1869–1942).

- *Vin Bravais,* created circa 1890 by the chemist Raoul Bravais in his laboratory at Asnières (near Paris), was sold until the early 1960s.

Lox poster, 1895, by
Georges Meunier
(1869–1942).
Courtesy of
J. Santo Domingo.

Kola-Coca poster, 1898, by K'lem. Courtesy of J. Santo Domingo.

Kola-Coca poster, ca. 1897, by Pal (1860–1942). Courtesy of J. Santo Domingo.

Mixed with Spanish wine, it contained 10 grams of coca leaves per liter and 15 grams of kola nut, guarana, caffeine, and cocoa. A poster was designed around 1890 by Eugène Ogé (1861–1936). It was available in granulated as well as elixir form, with the same active ingredients, the wine being replaced by curaçao.[4]

🙰 *Kola-Coca*, based on cinchona with coca and kola, contained no alcohol and was created by J. Genty at Chartres. We know of two

Quina-Coca poster, 1900,
by Louis Adolphe d'Auvergne
(1850–?). Courtesy of
J. Santo Domingo.

posters: one in from 1898 by K'lem around 1900 and the another from 1897 by Pal (1860–1942).

🕮 *Quina-Coca* was created in Saint-Étienne by the distiller J. Girond around 1900. It ceased production in 1913. A poster was created by Louis Adolphe d'Auvergne (1850–?) around 1900.

🕮 *Vin Désiles,* marketed between 1894 and the early 1960s, was created by Dr. Alexander Choffé in Levallois-Perret (near Paris). It contained 14 grams of coca leaves per liter, 13 grams of cinchona, 11 grams of kola nuts, 18 grams of orange alcohol, and 3 grams of cocoa. The range of products included tablets, granules, liqueur, and flour. In 1898, a liqueur was marketed called Désiline, with the same composition as Vin Désiles. Advertising for these products was supported by a poster, designed in 1895, by Francisco Tamagno

The Time of Ordeals:
The Imitators

129

Vin Koto poster, 1914, by
Louis Mangin. Courtesy of
J. Santo Domingo.

(1851–1933), as well as a series of postcards and color menus illustrated by Jane Atché (1872–1937), Firmin Bouisset (1859–1925), Gaston-Gérard (1859–?), and Tamagno.[5]

🍃 *Koto*, "a powerful wine with Peruvian coca," was marketed on boulevard Beaumarchais in Paris. A poster was made for it in 1914 by Louis Mangin.

🍃 *Elixir Mondet* was an alcoholic herbal liqueur produced in Gap in the Hautes-Alpes. It was recommended for various medical indications, such as fatigue or anemia, and as an anthelmintic for children. It contained lactophosphate of lime, yellow gentian, walnut

Elixir Mondet poster, ca. 1900,
anonymous.

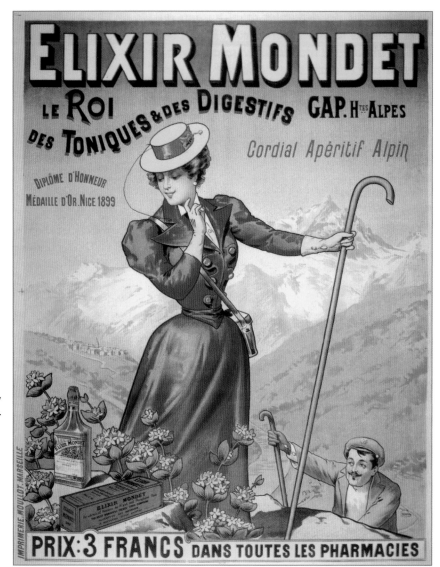

The Time of Ordeals:
The Imitators

leaf, and extracts from coca and kola. A poster by an anonymous artist was printed around 1900.

🙞 *Le Coq* was a wine-based restorative with coca and cinchona, made by Joseph Mercier, distiller in Redon (Ille et Vilaine). A poster was made around 1910 by Marcellin Auzolle (1862–1942).

🙞 *Sport,* a restorative tonic wine, was a "pleasant aperitif made with coca and kola" and manufactured by the distiller Auguste Ancel at Compiegne. A poster by an anonymous artist was printed around 1895.[6]

🙞 *Coca-Kola:* among the dozens of other wines and coca elixirs one could indeed find, at the Chapel pharmacy in Lyon, and from at least 1885, something called Coca-Kola—whose name and label graphics look suspiciously like a famous American drink that, as we shall see, will be created the following year in the United States: Coca-Cola.[7]

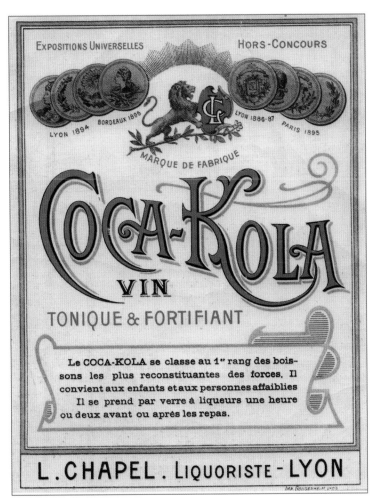

Coca-Kola label, ca. 1885.

The Rest of Europe

The rest of Europe would soon have its own array of coca products.

Belgium's notable products included: Vin Marin toni-nutritif, Vin tonique reconstituant, Vin tonique fortifiant, Vin Hann's, Vin Vital, Vin Richelle, and Vin tonique du Dr. Yonghi.

Of note in England:

Advertisement card for Vin du Dr. Rogé.

- *Hall's Coca Wine,* produced in London by Stephen Smith & Co., contained 17.8 percent alcohol and 0.003 percent alkaloids (4 milligrams of cocaine per wineglass) and was sold as a "great nervous restorer." It was described as tonic, "invaluable in the case of influenza, insomnia, neuralgia, anemia, mental fatigue, etc." A poster was designed in 1915 by Dudley Hardy (1867–1922).

- *Armbrecht's Coca Wine,* manufactured in London by the company Armbrecht, Nelson & Co. was used to fight against the "fatigue of mind and body." This "powerful nerve stimulant" was sold until 1923. One could choose among the Malaga with coca for ladies and children, Burgundy coca for gout, and Porto coca for dyspepsia, which came in at 15 percent alcohol and contained 0.006 percent alkaloids. The company also manufactured a "sparkling coca wine" and a "coca champagne."

- *Buckfast Tonic Wine,* was made by monks in Devon between 1897 and 1927. It contained maté, coca leaves, and vanilla. A decocainized version still exists today.

- *Marza Wine,* produced in London by Wright, Layman & Umney, came in at 17.5 percent alcohol and contained 0.001 percent alkaloids. It was recommended "for the development of brain, nerve, and muscle" and contained iron in addition to coca.

- *Savar's Coca Wine,* manufactured in 1876 in London and Liverpool by Evans Sons Lescher & Webb came in at 23.4 percent alcohol and contained 0.07 percent alkaloids.

- *Robinson's Coca Wine* was manufactured in Manchester by Benjamin Robinson. It came in at 16 percent acohol and contained the equivalent of 20 grams of coca leaves to every liter of port wine.

- *Coca Bynin,* with coca and malt, was developed in London by Allen and Hanburys Ltd. It came in at 10.7 percent alcohol and contained 0.025 percent alkaloids.[8]

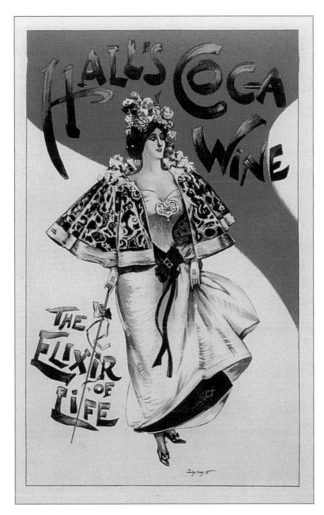

Hall's Coca Wine poster, 1915, by Dudley Hardy (1867–1922).

In Spain, the following products were available:

- *Vino Amargós* was made in Barcelona with cinchona, peptone, and coca leaves. One poster was designed around 1890 by Lluis Labarta (1852–1924).
- *Tonica Kola,* which at first was called *Nuez de Coca-Cola,* was produced in Ayelo near Valencia between 1880 and 1953. It contained coca leaves and kola nuts.
- *Vino con Coca del Peru* was sold by the pharmacist Trénard in Barcelona.
- *Vino y Nuez Coca Cola* was made at the Fabregas pharmacy in Barcelona.

The Time of Ordeals:
The Imitators

Vino Amargós poster, ca. 1890, by Lluis Labarta (1852–1924).

Coca Buton poster, 1906, anonymous.

Elixir Coca Buton poster, 1900, by
Adolfo Hohenstein (1854–1928).

Coca Buton advertising card.

Coca Buton poster, ca. 1900, by Jane Atché
(1872–1937). Courtesy of the Collection
Museo Nazionale Salce.

Cycling champions
Fausto Coppi and Gino Bartali
drinking Coca Buton
during Giro 1940.

Elixir Coca della Bolivia label by Fernet Branca.

In Italy the most famous coca wines were:

- *Vino Coca Buton,* manufactured in Bologna beginning in the early 1870s. It consisted of Bolivian coca leaves macerated in white wine. The company also made an *Elixir Coca Buton* that was aged six months. These preparations were still sold until very recently at the rate of 80,000 bottles per year. Posters (shown on the previous page) were commissioned from great Italian art nouveau poster artists such as Adolfo Hohenstein (1854–1928), Marcello Dudovich (1878–1962), Giovanni Mataloni (1869–1944), Ernesto Bottaro (1892–1936), and the French artist Jane Atché (1872–1937).[9]
- There was also *Elixir Coca della Bolivia* produced by Fernet Branca, and a *Coca Boliviana* by Bertocchini.

In the United States

Outside of France, it was in the United States that one could find the greatest quantity of coca-wine products. The plant and its therapeutic use were studied later than they were in France, so it was only in 1877 that the first coca-wine preparations were produced in the United States. Between the years 1890 and 1900, about twenty different coca wines were on the market.[10] Among them, notably:

- *Liebig's Co.'s Coca Beef Tonic,* a preparation made with coca, cinchona, iron, and alcohol at 24 percent, was produced in New York by the Liebig Company in 1880.
- *Coca Wine,* made in New York by Caswell, Hazard & Co. in 1880, came in at 15.35 percent alcohol and contained 118 milligrams of cocaine per bottle.
- *Wyomoke Tea* was a coca compound manufactured in Hartford, Connecticut, by Dr. Charles W. Scott and distributed by Shannon & Marwick, Proprietors, beginning in 1880.

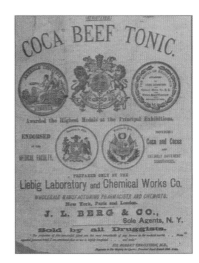

Advertisement for Liebig's Coca Beef Tonic.

Advertising card for Coca Wine, manufactured in New York by Caswell, Hazard & Co.

The Time of Ordeals: The Imitators

Advertisement for Metcalf's Coca Wine, 1910. Courtesy of James P. Musser.

🍂 *Beef, Wine and Coca,* manufactured by Sutcliff & Case in Peoria, Illinois, came in at 15 percent alcohol and contained 13 milligrams of cocaine per ounce. A 1913 analysis of a sample showed that in fact, it came in at 23.7 percent alcohol, contrary to what was announced, and that it contained 8.35 milligrams of cocaine per ounce.

🍂 *Metcalf's Coca Wine,* intended to fight "fatigue of mind or body," was prepared by Metcalf & Co. in Boston starting in 1877. It was a Malaga wine containing 21 percent alcohol and the equivalent of 9.7 milligrams of cocaine per ounce. It still existed in 1917.

🍂 *Maltine with Coca Wine* was made in New York by Maltine & Co. At one point it was selling 10,000 bottles per year and contained the equivalent of 9 milligrams of cocaine per ounce. Although the company announced its withdrawal in 1907, it still existed in 1917.

🍂 *Lambert's Wine of Coca* was produced in Detroit by Lambert & Co. It was composed of 22 percent alcohol with peptonate, iron, coca extract, and cod liver oil. It still existed in 1917.

🍂 *Cassebeer's Coca Calisaya* was made by Shepard & Co. in New York, who claimed that its product could sustain "one's vigor in the event of extreme physical exertion." It contained more than 40 percent alcohol and 0.10 percent coca. It still existed in 1917.

🍂 *Coca Cordial* was made in Detroit by Parke Davis in 1885. Every ounce contained the equivalent of the active ingredients in 4 grams of coca leaves.

🍂 *Pemberton's French Wine Coca* was certainly the most famous of these coca wines. Its first advertisement, in June 1884, described it as a: "superlative tonic and invigorator; a health restoring, strength giving, life sustaining prescription."[11]

The manufacturer of French Wine Coca was Dr. John S. Pemberton (1831–88) who, starting in 1869, owned a pharmaceutical laboratory in Atlanta, where he experimented with various plant and herbal preparations. One plant quickly drew his attention: coca. In March 1885, a reporter from the *Atlanta Journal* asked him about the medicinal properties of his new coca-based tonic. Pemberton explained the virtues of this plant. According to him: "It was first investigated by medical scientists of France, who have found the extract from the leaves, associated with pure wine, a most excellent invigorator of weak or

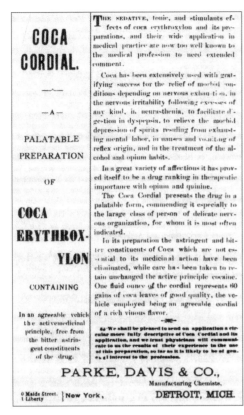

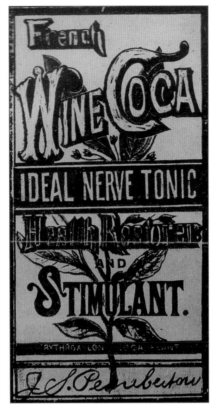

Advertisement for Coca Cordial.　　Pemberton's French Wine Coca label.

overworked constitutions." He admits that his drink was based on Vin Mariani:

> Mariani & Co., of Paris, prepare an exceedingly popular Wine of Coca.... I have observed very closely the most approved French formula, only deviating therefrom when assured by my own long experimentation and direct information from intelligent South American correspondents that I could improve upon [it]. I believe that I am now producing a better preparation than that of Mariani.[12]

The improvements that he mentioned in his interview consisted of the addition of two ingredients: the kola nut and damiana, the leaf of *Turnera diffusa,* which is used as an aphrodisiac. For him:

> The use of the coca plant not only preserves the health of all who use it, but prolongs life to a very great old age and enables the coca eaters to perform prodigies of mental and physical labor.[13]

John Pemberton (1831–88).

The Time of Ordeals:
The Imitators

139

Advertising placard for French Wine Coca.

According to Pemberton, among the constant users of coca, "instances are recorded of persons who have lived over 120, 130, 140 and even over 150 years!"[14]

Advertisements in local newspapers were increasing. In one of them we find this statement:

Americans are the most nervous people in the world. . . . All who are suffering from any nervous complaints we commend the use of that wonderful and delightful remedy, French Wine Coca, infallible in curing all who are afflicted with any nerve trouble, dyspepsia, mental and physical exhaustion, all chronic and wasting diseases, gastric irritability, constipation, sick headache, neuralgia etc. [. . .] Coca is a most wonderful invigorator of the sexual organs and will cure seminal weakness, impotency, etc., when all other remedies fail. To the unfortunate who are addicted to the morphine or opium habit, or the excessive use of alcoholic stimulants, the French Wine Coca has proven a great blessing.[15]

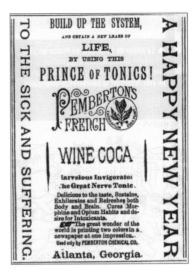

Advertisement for Pemberton's French Wine Coca in the *Atlanta Evening Capitol*, January 2, 1886.

Another ad announced that "888 bottles of Pemberton's French Wine Coca sold Saturday! It sells and proves a living joy to all who use it."[16]

The brand was registered May 19, 1885. Pemberton, appropriating Mariani's advertising methods, but without any evidence, soon claimed that his "French Wine Coca is endorsed by over 20,000 of the most learned and scientific medical men in the world!"

But laws prohibiting alcohol would jeopardize his product. Near the end of 1885, Atlanta passed such a law. Pemberton, fearing that French Wine Coca would have to be taken off the market, after much trial and error, replaced the wine and damiana with sugar syrup, citric acid, and caffeine mixed with soda. In spring 1886, the new drink was called Coca-Cola.

On June 28, 1887, Pemberton registered the trademark and the logo with the famous Spencerian script that contributed to his success, which is strangely similar to the image below and whose name is strangely similar to a French coca wine called Coca-Kola.

Label for Coca, manufactured by Girond.

The Time of Ordeals: The Imitators

French Wine Coca counter, Boston, 1899, in the *New England Druggist*, 1899.

With the end of prohibition in Atlanta in November 1887 sales of French Wine Coca resumed. At that time, an average of 720 bottles were sold per day.[17]

It is not known exactly when the production of French Wine Coca stopped. It was still for sale in 1899 in Boston, Massachusetts.[18]

Soon the phenomenal success of Coca-Cola, the "grandson" of Vin Mariani, born of an imitation, would in turn give birth to dozens of its own imitators.[19]

Coca-Cola, at that time, contained the equivalent of 8 milligrams of cocaine per glass. It was only in 1903 that the company began to decocainize the coca leaves, which are still used today in the formula. According to some sources, the Coca-Cola Company buys a hundred tons of coca leaves each year—mainly from Peru—for some 2.8 billion bottles and cans sold daily around the world. The Stepan Chemical Company, based in Maywood, New Jersey, is the only one authorized to decocainize coca leaves for the Coca-Cola Company.

Curiously, these days the company never mentions the coca included in its product, completely ignores its beginnings with French Wine Coca, and says even less about what it owes to Vin Mariani.

Several producers of coca wine simply added cocaine to their formulas. According to Mariani:

> Since the successful introduction of Vin Mariani to the medical profession of the United States, many druggists throughout the country have tried to make their own Coca preparations, but in every instance, physicians testing them have pronounced the same very disagreeable to the taste, and not only were they without efficacy, but even caused nausea, vomiting, and serious complications.[20]

His complaints against some of these rival preparations were justified by the methods used by their manufacturers. In a letter to the editor of the *New York Medical Journal* in 1885, Dr. William Oliver Moore complained about: "misquotations and substitutions" from several manufacturers of coca preparations, who had used quotations from his recent article published in the same journal about the effects of coca, "each in turn substituting the name of his own product instead of the one mentioned in the original," namely, Mariani's coca preparations, which he believed "to be the best among all those he had experimented."[21]

In the same issue there was a letter sent from an American doctor to Mariani offering to mention his name and his products very favorably in medical journals, for the modest sum of twenty-five dollars, a proposition that Mariani did not take up.[22]

In the same journal, two years later, Dr. Charles Fauvel, in a letter to the editor, states:

> The various notices appearing in journals and circulars quoting my name in connection with coca are entirely false and in every respect

Enameled metal advertisement for a competitor of Mariani called Kola-Coca. Courtesy of J. Santo Domingo.

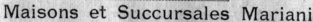
Information published by the Mariani Company concerning his plagiarism case.

a prevarication. The only preparation of coca employed by me with undoubted and uniform success has been the so well-known Vin Mariani, which, since 1865, I have had occasion to prescribe daily in my clinique, as well as, in my private practice.[23]

The methods of Mariani's rivals went even further. In 1903, a pharmacist in Marseilles, Antoine Mariani, taking advantage of having the same last name, cleverly launched on the market a Vin tonique A^ne Mariani à la coca du Pérou that he sold, misleadingly, in a bottle and with a label similar to the original.

To add to the public's confusion, Antoine Mariani went so far as to imitate the signature of Angelo Mariani on the bottle labels. The propagator of coca, reluctantly, had no choice but to take the plagiarist to court. On August 4, 1905, the Third Chamber of the Civil Tribunal of the Seine:

Jointly condemned a pharmacist from Marseilles and his Paris agent as guilty of fraudulent imitation of Vin Mariani, because of a similarity in the shape of the bottle, and similarity of the name, creating confusion with this product. It is established by this judgment that

The Time of Ordeals:
The Imitators

Advertisement for Apéritif Mariani Quinquina made by Antoine Mariani.

the brand: Vin Tonique Mariani à la Coca du Pèrou, belongs exclusively to Mr. Angelo Mariani, creator of the wine that bears his name, and Mr. Antoine Mariani can legally market his wine only by putting his first name Antoine before the name Mariani in letters of the same size and different colors for the two words.[24]

Counsel for the defendant stated that his closing argument might have been better if he had thought of drinking Vin Mariani just before: "not the Vin Mariani of my client, but the Vin Mariani of my opponent"![25]

The Time of Ordeals:
The Imitators

A few years later, in 1908, the same Antoine Mariani created the Apéritif Mariani Quinquina Company and launched an "Apéritif Mariani Quinquina," a "tonic wine with coca from Peru." The ownership of the company was divided into 2,500 shares of 100 francs each. Angelo Mariani had to issue a press release in February 1909 stating that he was absolutely not a party to the forming of the company.[26]

8 From Prescription to Prohibition

The Rise of Addiction, Anti-cocaine Laws
in the United States and France, and the
Last Years of Mariani's Company

In the United States

Between 1859, the year when Albert Niemann isolated cocaine, and 1884, the year when Karl Koller discovered its anesthetic properties, only two medical studies were published in 1874 and 1876 in the United States on this new molecule.[1] Later, the dozens of articles published in 1884–85 will describe cocaine as a "wonder drug," "a cure-all" medicine. Between July and December 1885 there were twenty-seven articles, letters, and notes on cocaine in *The New York Medical Journal* alone. The therapeutic indications included its use as an anesthetic in surgery, as a tonic in neurology for nervous diseases, as a treatment for respiratory diseases such as asthma, sinusitis, or hay fever, and finally as a treatment for morphine addiction.

But very quickly in the medical press, the first articles appeared describing undesirable toxic effects in some patients during surgical operations due to cocaine overdosing by surgeons. Other articles would follow warning against the risks of habitual usage and addiction.

The mainstream press echoed these concerns: in November 1885 the *New York Times* described the case of America's first known cocaine abuser, Dr. Charles D. Bradley, a prominent doctor in Chicago, "who

147

Sketch in *Hampton's Magazine*, May 1911.

DAILY OUR CHILDREN ARE EXPOSED TO THE LURE OF COCAINE IN INNOCENT-SEEMING SODA FOUNTAIN PREPARATIONS.

has become crazed from excessive indulgence in cocaine." He ruined his health, his career, and his marriage, lost all his property, and was finally arrested for assaulting a drugstore clerk who refused to sell him cocaine.[2]

William Halsted, one of America's greatest surgeons, first at Bellevue Hospital in New York, then professor of surgery at the John Hopkins University School of Medicine, experimented with cocaine too. He and three of his colleagues injected cocaine repeatedly during their researches on its anesthetic effects. Halsted spent the rest of his life addicted, curing his cocaine addiction with morphine.[3]

We can also mention the name of the neurologist William Hammond, former surgeon general of the army, who was a fervent cocaine user. He is known for having maintained that cocaine was no more harmful than tea or coffee and that he had never heard of a single case of addiction.

From Prescription to Prohibition

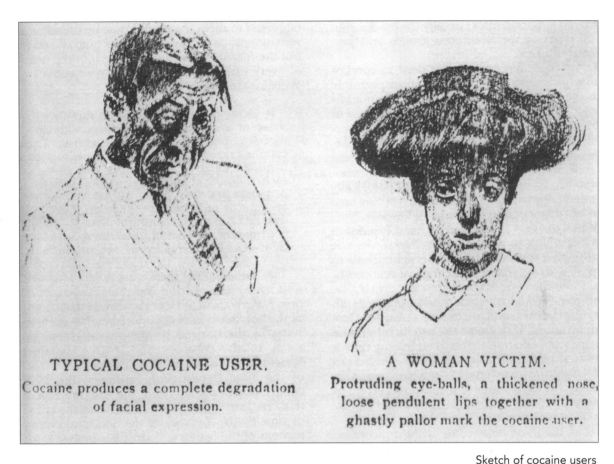

TYPICAL COCAINE USER.
Cocaine produces a complete degradation
of facial expression.

A WOMAN VICTIM.
Protruding eye-balls, a thickened nose,
loose pendulent lips together with a
ghastly pallor mark the cocaine user.

Sketch of cocaine users
in *Hampton's Magazine*,
May 1911.

Soon the press reported several cases of people with cocaine habits, but these remained for a decade largely confined to the medical world and more particularly to men.[4]

Despite this, and perhaps because the use of cocaine began to spread among the population, American states would begin to enact prohibition laws, though in an unsystematic way. The first was Oregon, which on February 21, 1887, banned the sale and possession of cocaine without a prescription. The second was Montana in March 1889, followed by New York in 1893 (but only partially because lawmakers only banned prescription refills without banning over-the-counter sales), then Colorado and Illinois in 1897. In 1898 it was the turn of Massachusetts and Louisiana. Between 1899 and 1905, seven other states would follow.

The anti-cocaine campaign doubled in intensity around the end of the nineteenth century and the beginning of the twentieth. Perhaps an explanation for this can be found in these words written by Dr. Thomas Crothers in 1898:

From Prescription
to Prohibition

Persons of the tramp and low criminal classes who use this drug are increasing in many of the cities. The cheapness and ease with which the drug can be obtained and the relief of pain and discomfort which follows its use make it very popular among this class.[5]

According to Crothers the prices of cocaine at this date were indeed low as it could be obtained at around two dollars an ounce.

Cocaine was first used as a stimulant by manual laborers, especially dockworkers in New Orleans and along the Mississippi River. Since the labor was hard, many of these workers were black. It was also used by railroad workers and agricultural laborers. In the mining states of Ohio and Colorado, cocaine was used by miners to sustain their hard work. The same was also the case among workers in the textile mills of Connecticut and Maine.

Cocaine then became an urban vice that spread through the underworld, first in southern cities. New Orleans, according to reports, counted thousands of cocaine fiends, mostly poorer blacks and prostitutes, both black and white. Cities like Dallas, Atlanta, and Houston were reporting cocaine epidemics. In New York, in a report published in 1903 by the American Pharmaceutical Association, the city police commissioner stated bluntly that "the classes of the community most addicted to the habitual use of cocaine are the parasites who live on the earnings of prostitutes of the lowest order, and young degenerates who acquire the habit through their connection with prostitutes and parasites." Major medical journals and popular magazines soon became filled with articles that linked cocaine with crime, especially within the black population in southern states.[6] The American Pharmaceutical Association issued a statement in 1902 that there were at least 200,000 cocaine users in the country. According to a questionable figure, *The Canadian Pharmaceutical Journal,* quoting a statistic by the American Bureau of Chemistry, stated that in 1909 there were "6,000,000 cocaine victims in the United States"[7]

The movies adopted the theme. About fifteen silent films, made between 1909 and 1928, deal with cocaine.

Among these were two medium-length films: first, *For His Son* (1912), by the great director D. W. Griffith. The film tells the story of a pharmacist who, in order to help his son financially, invented a soft drink mixed with cocaine, Dopokoke. The drink meets with huge success, but the downside is that his son gets to like it, discovers its active

Cover illustration by Henri Gazan (1887–1960), for the magazine *L'Animateur des Temps Nouveaux,* July 25, 1930. On it, Benjamin Franklin is quoted as having said, "It's more expensive to maintain a vice than to raise two children." By this time in history cocaine is seen as a detriment to society in both America and France.

Poster for the cocaine movie
The Pace That Kills, 1928.

ingredient, cocaine, to which he quickly becomes addicted and dies of an overdose.

The second film, *The Mystery of the Leaping Fish* (1916), by John Emerson with a screenplay by Tod Browning, relates the comic adventures of the detective Coke Ennyday, played by the great actor Douglas Fairbanks. In charge of an investigation aimed at dismantling a network of opium traffickers, Coke Ennyday solves the case with the help of cocaine, which he either injects repeatedly with a collection of syringes carried on his belt or snorts from a full salad bowl.[8]

From Prescription
to Prohibition

151

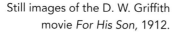
Still images of the D. W. Griffith movie *For His Son*, 1912.

Famous actors such as Errol Flynn and actresses such as Norma Talmadge, Mabel Normand, and Tallulah Bankhead developed cocaine habits, often leading to lurid scandals. Tallulah Bankhead was quoted as saying "Cocaine is not habit-forming. I've been taking it for years, and I should know."

In his novel *The Girl from Hollywood* (1923) Edgar Rice Burroughs

Douglas Fairbanks as the detective Coke Ennyday in *The Mystery of the Leaping Fish* (1916) by John Emerson.

From Prescription
to Prohibition

depicted cocaine habits in Hollywood. Cocaine also influenced music. Blues and jazz singers, among them Ella Fitzgerald, recorded songs on this topic in the late twenties and in the thirties.[9]

Pharmaceutical companies would soon be criticized for the danger posed by some of their products that had high doses of cocaine. In the United States, total cocaine consumption, imported and domestically manufactured, rose from 850 kilos in 1890 to nearly 9 tons in 1903. It has to be noted that at this date the quantity of imported cocaine had declined with the increase of the cocaine manufacturing capacities of American companies.[10] Indeed it soon ranked in value among the top five products made by U.S. pharmaceutical companies. In 1900 eight major pharmaceutical and chemical companies were manufacturing cocaine in the States: Parke Davis; Squibb; Mallinckrodt; McKesson and Robbins; Scheiffelin and Company; Powers-Weightman-Rosengarten; New York Quinine and Chemical Works; and the American branch of Merck. The patent medicines containing cocaine were used mainly to cure tobacco addiction, asthma, and nasal catarrh. Among the most popular on the market:

    Coca-Bola, developed by Dr. Charles Mitchell of Philadelphia, was a chewing gum aimed at curing tobacco addiction. It contained 710 milligrams of cocaine per ounce (each piece of gum would

Advertisement for Coca-Bola chewing gum.

Advertisement for Dr. Tucker's Asthma Specific.

contain the equivalent of several lines of cocaine!). One could also mention: *Tobacco Bullets,* manufactured by the Victor Remedy Company in Dayton, Ohio; *Wonder Workers,* manufactured by George S. Beck of Springfield, Ohio; and *Dr. Elder's Celebrated Tobacco Specific,* manufactured in St. Joseph, Missouri.

Dr. Tucker's Asthma Specific, created in 1889 and manufactured in Mount Gilead, Ohio, was sold with a spray bottle to use as a nasal spray to treat asthma and hay fever. It contained atropine and between 230 and 450 milligrams of cocaine per ounce (i.e., between 1 gram and 1.8 grams per bottle). Between 50,000 and 80,000 units were sold yearly. It was still marketed in the 1930s.

Dr. Birney's Catarrhal Powder, manufactured in Chicago beginning in 1893, was designed to treat inflammation of the mucous membranes of the nose and throat. It contained between 1.10 percent and 4 percent cocaine, according to the analysis, therefore 585 to 1,250 milligrams per ounce. A decocainized version was released in 1907 without any success. In the earliest known confession by a female addict, Annie Meyers describes her descent "from a well-balanced Christian woman" to "a haggard and wretched physical and mental wreck." According to her all her problems began with Birney's Catarrhal Powder used to cure a severe cold.[11]

Advertisement for Dr. Birney's Catarrhal Powder. Courtesy of the Wisconsin Historical Society.

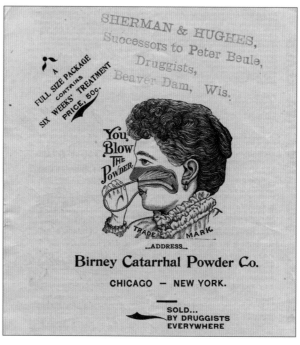

Anticatarrhal cocaine products.

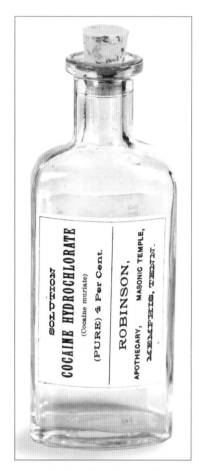

Bottle of a solution of cocaine hydrochlorate.

🙤 *Ryno's Hay Fever and Catarrh Remedy,* developed in Wayland, Michigan, was recommended for flu, hay fever, and stuffy nose; it was composed of 99.95 percent cocaine! One could also cite: *Az-Ma-Syde, Dr. Einhorn's Asthma-Spray, Dr. Cole's Catarrh Cure, Dr. Gray's Catarrh Powder, Crown Catarrh Powder,* and *Dr. Agnew's Catarrh Powder.* These patent medicines were among the most diverted from their intended use, becoming much sought-after medicines by cocaine fiends who compulsively consumed several bottles a day.[12]

Most of these preparations faced legal action, not for the cocaine they contained, but because they omitted reporting its existence on their boxes and bottles! Other products with cocaine included suppositories, eye and tooth drops, gargles, and lozenges.

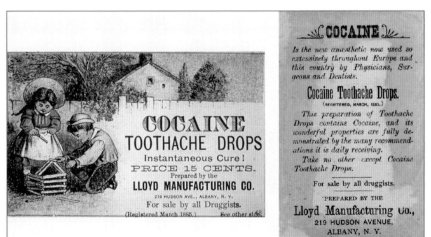

Advertisement for Cocaine Toothache Drops registered by Lloyd Manufacturing Co. in 1885.

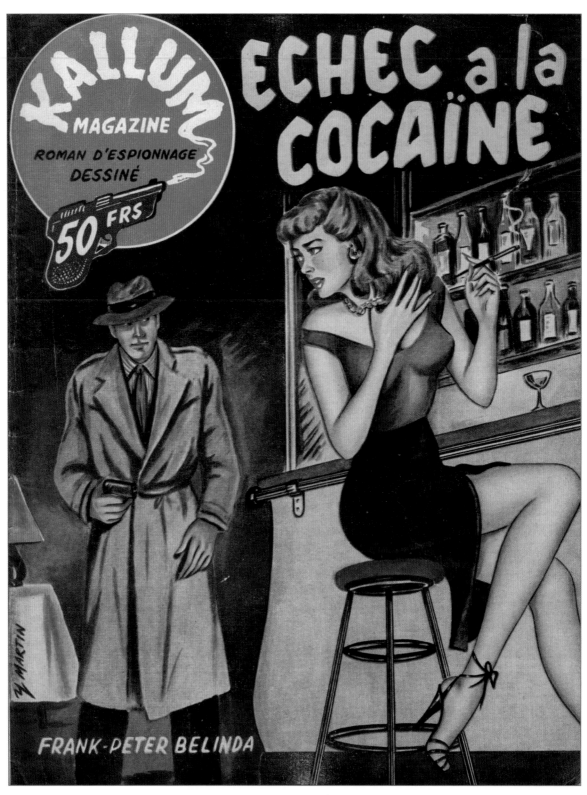

Cover illustration by Yves Martin for the pulp novel *Echec à la cocaïne*
(Cocaine breakdown) by Frank-Peter Belinda, 1953.

Vin Mariani was also soon to be criticized or even sued. As early as 1890, Dr. Austin Flint, professor of physiology at the Bellevue Hospital Medical College in New York, published an article in *Medical News* on the "The Effrontery of Proprietary Medicine Advertisers," in which he criticized the methods of the Mariani Company. He accused the company of distributing advertising flyers praising their products, such as Vin Mariani, with the name of the Bellevue Hospital as a heading followed by a list of 142 doctors recommending it. In its right of reply, the Mariani Company wrote that it had permission from each of the doctors to use their names, and added that it had available to anyone who wanted them more than 7,000 letters from doctors who used or prescribed Vin Mariani. The right of reply concludes, in a somewhat taunting manner, that Dr. Flint and his father, also a prominent doctor,

> have for years, ordered Vin Mariani for use in their own family, as well as largely for their patients and this we can and will attest by prescriptions and letters bearing the name of Austin Flint, M.D., which we hold subject to inspection.

The Mariani Company distributed a pamphlet with the above documents and two articles favorable to their product.[13]

In October 1894, the chemist Charles Fennel of the Pure Food Commission of the State of Ohio placed Vin Mariani on a list of some one hundred adulterated products thereby in violation of a decree of March 20, 1884. This product did not, according to him, meet the required standards, particularly with regard to its main ingredient, coca leaves, of which he doubted the amount of two ounces indicated by the manufacturer. He even filed a lawsuit and had a prominent Cincinnati pharmacist arrested for selling Vin Mariani. The commission lost its case. Charles Fennel had to retract and admit that he made a mistake by not referring to the latest edition of the *United States Dispensatory*, which included the whole U.S. Pharmacopoeia and authorized Vin Mariani. He therefore had to remove it from the list of products under investigation and authorized its sale once again. Dozens of American medical journals relayed the news. Mariani published some of these articles in a booklet.[14]

In July 1903, at the request of the state Board of Health of Pennsylvania, Professor Samuel Sadtler and Dr. F. A. Genth, chemists in

Philadelphia, analyzed the contents of bottles of Vin Mariani to determine if the wine contained cocaine and would therefore contravene the act of April 22, 1903, that regulated the sale or prescription of cocaine preparations. Analyses by both chemists showed that Vin Mariani contained an infinitesimal quantity of cocaine (about .010 to .013 of 1 percent) and concluded that its presence is "incidental to its manufacture and not intentional [. . .] and too small to lead to the suspicion of cocaine, as such, having been added to obtain its medicinal effects." The attorney general of Pennsylvania concluded his report by stating that Vin Mariani does not violate the act because it is a preparation:

> Made of a pure French Bordeaux wine, representing in addition the aromatic and desirable properties of two ounces of fresh coca leaves, carefully selected with reference to their minimum alkaloid properties.[15]

Cover illustration by A. Buguet for the pulp novel *Cocaïne* by Pierre Sorel, 1924.

On February 3, 1905, at a meeting of its directors, the American Medical Association established an advisory committee, the Council on Pharmacy and Chemistry. The purpose of this council was to examine the composition of the various medicinal preparations not included in the Pharmacopoeia of the United States and to set standards for drug manufacturing and advertising. Preparations had to comply with ten specific rules.

Commenting on the new regulations, Mariani noted that:

> The spirit in which this work has been planned is excellent, and if it proves successful in driving from the market a host of nondescript nostrums which are inflicted upon the public and upon dealers it will be a lasting benefit to humanity. [. . .] Imitators following upon the success of Vin Mariani have attempted to foist upon the profession so-called Coca-wines extemporaneously prepared from cocaine and cheap grades of wine.[16]

Mariani, tired of these attacks and false accusations coming only from the United States against his product, decided to offer:

> A reward of $1,000 for the arrest and conviction of any person circulating malicious falsehoods, or libelous and defamatory reports

Cover of *Détective*,
March 21, 1929.

intended to discredit the old established reputation of this house or the integrity of Vin Mariani.[17]

On June 30, 1906, President Roosevelt signed the Pure Food and Drug Act. This legislation superseded many ineffective national laws by establishing the Pharmacopoeia of the United States as a legal standard. Its objective was to prevent: "the manufacture, sale, or transportation of adulterated or misbranded or poisonous or deleterious foods, drugs, medicines, and liquors [. . .]." The Pure Food and Drug Act is the first major consumer-protection law. It stipulated that patent medicines had to list their ingredients on the labels of their products.[18]

From Prescription
to Prohibition

Cover illustration of the sheet music for *Cocaïne ou conseils à un ami*, 1921.

Mariani complied. The new labels on bottles of Vin Mariani sold in the United States after that date specify the content: 17 percent alcohol and the words: "Each ounce represents one-tenth of one grain of cocaine."[19] That it to say, 110 milligrams per bottle.

According to various sources and analyses of the time, some dating back to 1877, a bottle of Vin Mariani would contain the equivalent of 110 to 132 milligrams of cocaine per bottle.[20] Two glasses of Bordeaux of Vin Mariani, the prescribed daily dose, should therefore contain the equivalent of about 50 to 70 milligrams of cocaine, which corresponds roughly to snorting a line of cocaine, depending of course on its size and the purity of the product.[21]

Mariani asserted repeatedly that: "no matter in how large doses taken, Vin Mariani has NEVER produced cocainism." Likewise, several articles in the company's American journal, *Mariani's Coca Leaf,* denounce both the confusion that occurs between cocaine and coca and the addition of cocaine to some medicinal preparations, which, as is specified, is not the case with Vin Mariani. The Mariani Company also made clear that its wine contained only the most aromatic varieties of coca leaves, with the lowest alkaloid content, including cocaine.[22] To our knowledge, no cases of dependence on, or poisoning from, Vin Mariani were reported in the medical literature of the time.

Also in 1906, a subcommittee of the Council on Pharmacy and Chemistry examined samples of Mariani's wine. The committee's report was published on November 26 in the *Journal of the American Medical Association.* The report stated that an analysis had been performed on samples of Vin Mariani, "a preparation of red wine, apparently imported from Bordeaux, and fortified, in this country, by an alcoholic preparation of coca leaves or other parts of the coca plant," and to which was added 6 percent sugar and came in at 16.15 percent alcohol.

This product, according to the report, violated two of the ten rules promulgated at the February 3, 1905 meeting. Rule 5 stated: "No article will be admitted or retained, concerning which the manufacturer or his agents make misleading statements as to geographical source, raw material from which made, or method of collection, or preparation." The report estimates that the Mariani Company is ambiguous about the origin of the product. The medical journal, in its analysis of the report, estimated that Vin Mariani: "as imported is simply an ordinary cheap French wine, the preparation sold in this country as Vin Mariani being compounded in this

Cover of *Police Magazine,*
December 14, 1930.

country. Yet the advertising literature, the label on the bottle, state directly or indirectly that it is a French preparation." Their aim was: "evidently intended to convey the impression that it is imported." This argument, in our opinion, is particularly specious since Mariani always maintained that his Vin Mariani was composed of a Bordeaux imported from France and extracts of coca leaves, which were then combined and bottled at his factory in New York.

The product, according to the report, also violated Rule 6, which stated: "No article will be admitted or retained of which the manufacturer or his agents make unwarranted exaggerated or misleading statements as

From Prescription
to Prohibition

Cover illustration by Paul Thiriat for the pulp novel *Les Drames de la cocaïne* (Cocaine tragedies) by Guy de Teramond, 1929.

Advertisement in the *Practical Druggist and Review of Reviews*, August 1907.

The MERITS OF OUR COCAINE

as a first-class, thoroughly reliable preparation have long since been fully recognized by the majority of physicians, surgeons and chemists, and more especially has it been distinguished by the approbation of

Dr. Carl Koller, New York (Formerly of Vienna, the first to apply Cocaine in medicine)
Dr. B. H. Paul, London
Prof. Dr. Schroetter, Vienna
Prof. Stoerk, Vienna
Prof. Stellwag, Vienna
Prof. Dr. Jurasz, Heidelberg

Prof. Dr. E. Fischer, Berlin
Prof. Dr. Riedinger, Wurzburg
Prof. Dr. G. Dragendorf, Dorpat
Dr. K. Emele, Graz
Dr. Leopold Landau, Berlin
Dr. Herrnheiser, Prague
Prof. Casimiro Manessei, Rome

Dr. G. B. Dantone, Rome
Dr. Aug. Ritter von Reuss, Vienna
Prof. Dr. Schoebe, Prague
Prof. Dr. U. Mosso, Turin
Prof. M. A. Tichomiroff, Moscow
Dr. W. Golden Mortimer, New York (Author of the most exhaustive Monograph on Coca)

WHEN ORDERING Cocaine Hydrochlorate from your jobber, specify "Boehringer" or "B. & S." It will cost no more than any other brand and is supplied in all size packages.

Chem. Pure, Large Crystals
Chem. Pure, Small Silky Crystals (Flakes)
Chem. Pure, Powder

C. F. BOEHRINGER & SOEHNE
7 CEDAR STREET, NEW YORK
LARGEST MAKERS IN THE WORLD OF QUININE AND COCAINE
WRITE FOR DESCRIPTIVE PRICE LIST

From Prescription to Prohibition

to therapeutic value." The report mentioned the list of ailments treated by Vin Mariani that appeared on the promotional materials of the company. It concluded that Vin Mariani was a beverage rather than a medicine.

The medical journal, in its analysis of the report, questioned the authenticity of the many glowing testimonials published by the Mariani Company.[23] Again, the criticism seems unjustified given that Mariani, as we have seen, got these authentic testimonials without financial compensation. When asked, "it must cost you an awful lot of money for all these endorsements," Mariani used to answer humorously:

> It has cost me a life's work. For nearly half a century I have been striving to merit praise for a panacea for tired brains and fatigued muscles. Vin Mariani has achieved success and my reward comes UNSOLICITED, without money as it is without price.[24]

An American advertisement featuring the testimony of writer Emile Zola.

In 1907 the Massachusetts State Board of Health stated in its annual report that it had examined 175 patent medicines in search of cocaine. Thirty contained cocaine, among which twenty-one were coca wines. Among them was Vin Mariani.[25]

Because of all these reports and no doubt to reassure its customers, the same year, in a circular sent to retail pharmacies on May 9, 1907, the Mariani Company noted:

> In answer to many inquiries from physicians and druggists, we beg to advise you that Vin Mariani is now, by furthering our special processing, *entirely free of cocaine.* This has been deemed advisable because of uncertainty through confounding Vin Mariani with preparations classified under cocaine regulations. Since the first introduction of Vin Mariani, nearly half a century ago, we have emphasized our use

Illustration by Marcel Vertès (1895–1961) in F. Carco's *Rue Pigalle*, 1927.

N° 110 - 1ᵉʳ Janvier 1933. **1 fr.** **Tous les Dimanches.**

POLICE
MAGAZINE

LES POURVOYEURS DE COCO

Lire, pages 8 et 9, nos révélations troublantes sur le trafic de la cocaïne à Paris et l'existence des odieux pourvoyeurs de drogue. La jeune femme ci-dessus prépare un paquet de coco qu'elle enfermera dans cet innocent bouquet, afin de dépister les vigilants inspecteurs de la brigade mondaine. (S. G. P.)

Cover of *Police Magazine*,
January 1, 1933.

of Coca chosen for aromatic and medicinal qualities and, as we have never considered the negligible content of alkaloid in such leaves essential to our formula, and to entirely remove all misapprehension, our processing *now completely eliminates it;* otherwise Vin Mariani continues of the high standard so long favorably known to the medical profession—i.e., An imported French Bordeaux wine with a special processing of leaves of Erythroxylon Coca.[26]

In 1909, Connecticut banned the sale of coca wine without a prescription. The ban stated that if the "coca wine contains cocaine, as it should, it comes under the cocaine law requiring a physician's prescription. If on the other hand, it contains no cocaine, as is stated on the label of Vin Mariani, it is misbranded."[27]

From Prescription
to Prohibition

THE DOPE-FIENDS.

Dr. Wilson—Don't be alarmed, gentlemen. We won't take it from you all at once. We'll taper you down gradually, and after a while you'll have confidence enough in yourselves to get along without it.

Sketch by Samuel Erhart (1862–1937) in *Puck,* September 11, 1912.

While the Pure Food and Drug Act had finally limited the use of cocaine in medicinal preparations, it had not settled the question of the sale of cocaine itself. Indeed, as noted by the American historian Joseph Spillane, as long as cocaine met the standards of purity and it was labeled correctly, there was no federal restriction on its sale. The error of legislators was "in making little distinction among various cocaine products or between cocaine and the coca-leaf from which it came." Probably out of ignorance. This approach, he says, has had a devastating impact on the control of cocaine, because it helped to eradicate a flourishing coca business "that presented no great threat to public health while leaving cocaine production virtually untouched. By driving low-potency cocaine products off the market entirely, the field was left wide open to the sale of pure cocaine."[28]

The Harrison Narcotics Tax Act of December 17, 1914, would go further, requiring that those who produce, import, manufacture, or distribute coca-leaf preparations register, pay a fee, and keep a register of

Cover illustration by Jean Saunier for the pulp novel *Les Forçats de la neige* (Snow slaves) by M. Nadaud and A. Fage, 1926.

sales. Section 6 of the Act states that: "the provisions of this Act shall not apply to decocainized coca leaves or preparations made therefrom, or to other preparations of coca leaves which do not contain cocaine."

In 1917 a study showed that there were still seventeen alcoholic coca-based and/or cocaine preparations for sale in U.S. pharmacies, including Vin Mariani, the only one to be included in its decocainized version.[29]

From Prescription to Prohibition

In France

In France too, between 1859, the year when Albert Niemann isolated cocaine, and 1884, the year when Karl Koller discovered its anesthetic properties, there were only two medical studies on cocaine published and those were in 1868 and 1869, six years earlier than in the United States.[30]

Illustration by Louis Bonnotte (1890–1954) in *Fantasio*, December 16, 1933.

LES PARADIS ARTIFICIELS : LA FEMME EN PROIE A LA COCAÏNE

Composition de BONNOTTE

But in 1884–85 alone, dozens of articles and studies were published on the subject, as well as twelve theses. The first therapeutic indications were in ophthalmology, dental surgery, otorhinolaryngology, urology, obstetrics, and treatment for morphine addiction.

The first cases of chronic intoxication and more specifically their psychic manifestations were described in 1889.[31]

But cocaine would become a public health issue only around 1910, a decade later than in the United States, with the development of nasal inhalation. Cocaine was very common in bohemian circles, the underworld, and the demimonde. According to two psychiatrists at the Saint Anne Lunatic Asylum, Drs. Briand and Vinchon, over 50 percent of the women frequenting Montmartre nightclubs in 1912 were cocaine addicts.[32]

Cocaïnomane

Drawing of a cocaine addict, 1930, by Jules Isnard Dransy (1883–1945). Courtesy of Ronald K. Siegel.

From Prescription to Prohibition

Watercolor by Leonette Cappiello (1875–1942).

The *New York Times* correspondent in France, in an article entitled "Paris Fears Growth of Cocaine Craze," described the Montmartre cafés:

Women seated before a glass of port or liqueur with a little gold or enameled box like a snuffbox beside them, from which they take from time to time a pinch of the pernicious white crystals and inhale them feverishly.

The journalist noticed that, "in the neighborhood of Montmarte are now a large number of cocaine merchants, who successfully carry on the business under the very eyes of the police." He adds that:

A remarkable feature of the cocaine trade is the regular rise in the price every night as the supplies begin to run short. The Parisienne, who can only get a small amount at a time, will commence by paying $1 a gram before dinner, and an hour or two after midnight will pay $8 or $10 for the same quantity, which is generally adulterated.

He quotes the testimony of the two psychiatrists, Briand and Vinchon, from the Saint Anne Lunatic Asylum, who noticed that: "There is now a veritable epidemic of the cocaine habit, with the sinister result of the arrival every day at the now-overcrowded Saint Anne Asylum of patients whose reason has been sapped by this poison."[33]

During the Great War cocaine became a propaganda weapon. The mainstream press denounced cocaine as "a German war weapon" and "the Boche poison." Doctors Courtois-Suffit and R. Giroux, authors in 1918 of one of the first comprehensive studies of cocaine as well as of numerous

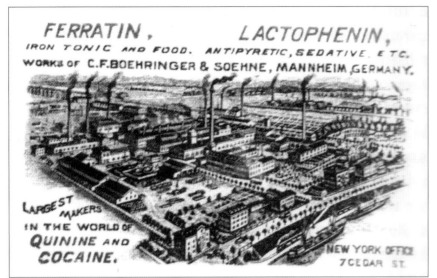

Advertisement for the Boehringer factory.

Drawing by Jean Camille Bellaigue (1893–1931) in *La Charrette charrie*, December 1923.

NUMÉRO 24.
Deuxième Année.

LE NUMÉRO : 1 Fr. 25
Étranger : 1 Fr. 75.

La Charrette
"charrie"

aujourd'hui

LA COCO

Dessins de J.-C. BELLAIGUE
Texte par CYRIL-BERGER, José GERMAIN,
André WARNOD et Michel HERBERT

Cover illustration by Jean Camille Bellaigue (1893–1931)
for the magazine *La Charrette charrie*, December 1923.

articles on the subject, advanced the notion that, "the German traffic was so important before the war that one could compare it to a 'toxic offensive.'"[34] Germany, with the Merck and Boehringer laboratories, was at the time the world's largest producer of cocaine.

"Coco" (cocaine in French slang) would become the drug of choice during the Roaring Twenties.

People from all backgrounds and social categories were affected. Among them were artists and writers. The influence of cocaine on artistic and literary creation has never really been studied in comparison, for

Cover illustration by Léon Pousthomis (1881–1916) of the sheet music for *La coco*, 1914.

Scene from the film *Barrabas*
by Louis Feuillade, 1919.

instance, with the numerous studies published on opium. Writers would take up the subject, and among the best known were Francis Carco, Pierre Mac Orlan, Philippe Soupault, Joseph Kessel, René Crevel, Robert Desnos, Victor Margueritte, Jean Cocteau, and Marcel Proust.[35] Writers such as Guy de Maupassant, Pierre Louÿs, Claude Farrère, Antonin Artaud, Joe Bousquet, Roger Vailland, Jacques Rigaut, and Roger Gilbert-Lecomte were cocaine users.

The *chanteuses réalistes* (realistic singers) Fréhel, Nitta Jo, La Palma, Gina Manes, and Emma Liébel sang about or consumed cocaine. Silent film also addressed the theme.[36]

Some painters, like Modigliani, Francis Picabia, and Yves Tanguy, were users of it as well.

With regard to the artists, the doctors Courtois-Suffit and R. Giroux went so far as to wonder if cocaine had not produced in them "a special deformation of their conception, a general aberration of the senses and more particularly of vision and hearing." The two doctors had a very original theory about the genesis of modern art:

> We were quickly convinced that by sensory disorders, in particular of sight and hearing and also by the hallucinations and psychic disturbances brought about by the drug , that cocaine addiction had in recent years a strange and unfortunate impact in various fields of art. And considering some imaginatively peculiar productions both in painting and music, we feel entitled to think that the use of cocaine is sufficient to explain them. It also seems that cocaine addiction played an important role in the emergence of Dadaism.[37]

In 1924, in *La coco poison moderne* (Cocaine, A Modern Poison), V. Cyril and Dr. Berger go even further. If they admit that some leaders of the Cubism movement are sincere and are not drug addicts, it is not the case for others whom they call "cocaine drunkards," and that one encounters among them:

> Those who try to outdo the Cubists, the Dadaists, the impotent, the willing fools who cannot be original other than by a carefully studied eccentricity in their attitudes, who replace music with blaring horns

Illustration *La neige* (Snow), by Yan Bernard Dyl (1887–1944), in Pierre Mac Orlan *La danse macabre*, 1927.

From Prescription to Prohibition

Cover illustration by Jack Roberts
of the sheet music for
Madame Coco, 1924.

and typewriters, and painting with any incongruity stuck on a canvas, and drama with the scandal of some lewd exhibitions announced with a lot of publicity.[38]

In 1924, according to highly questionable figures from the police, there were no less than 80,000 cocaine addicts in Paris.[39]

The evolution of regulation would be more gradual and would start later in France than in the United States. The public authorities reacted by enacting a law on poisonous substances on July 12, 1916, and implementing a decree of application on September 14, 1916. It classified these substances into three categories: Table A includes ordinary poisons, Table C includes hazardous products, and Table B includes narcotics, among which cocaine was listed. Coca was not mentioned. But the law would not solve the problem of trafficking and would not stop the consumption of cocaine. Arrests quadrupled between 1916 and 1921, from 53 to 212. In 1921, doctors M. Courtois-Suffit and R. Giroux warned again about the risk of a new epidemic. They noted that "the traffic has expanded and the legislation is far from achieving the goal that the lawmaker had set. Paris is no longer the sole center of drug trafficking [. . .] today, the vice has invaded the provinces." According to them, much of the trafficking was carried out by demobilized French soldiers or U.S. occupation forces stationed in Germany who were lured by the significant profits found in coming to France to sell cocaine. They could buy it in Germany at 300 to 500 francs per kilogram and sell it in France at between 10 and 15 francs per gram. . . . The *New York Times* in an article entitled, "Soldiers Smuggle Cocaine to French," relayed the information.[40]

The law of July 13, 1922, toughened the penalties provided by the 1916 law, in particular with regard to the right to search public places without a warrant.

The International Convention on Narcotic Drugs, concluded at Geneva on February 19, 1925, further requested that the contracting parties control "all officinal and non-officinal preparations [. . .] containing [. . .] more than 0.10 percent cocaine." The Convention was ratified by France, in the law of June 19, 1927. The decree of March 20, 1930, added coca leaves to Table B as well as preparations, including coca wine, containing more than 0.10 percent cocaine.

The pharmacists L. G. Toraude and E. Dufau noted in a May 1931 article on the issue of coca in light of the decree, that in the latest French

... Tel est pris, qui croyait la prendre...

La Dernière prise (The last sniff), by Jean Camille Bellaigue (1893–1931), in La Charrette charrie, December 1923.

Codex, there is no reference to any dosing method, and no titration is set for these different products:

> The French pharmacist is unable to know with any certainty, in an official and verifiable manner [. . .] what pharmaceutical forms of coca-leaf preparations are subject to the decree of 1930.[41]

In an article published two months later, the authors returned to the issue by analyzing the consequences of the decision of the Ministry of Public Health, which had just been published on July 7, 1931. Regarding the coca leaf and its preparations, pharmacies were allowed to use, without constraint, an annual allowance of 5 kilos of leaves. "As for their use [. . .] a dose of 60 grams of leaves [. . .] necessary for making a liter of coca wine, is not subject to any regulation." With respect to the labeling of cocaine preparations, the dose exempted from regulation is 1 gram of cocaine per 1,000.[42]

From Prescription to Prohibition

A new international Convention on Narcotic Drugs, concluded at Geneva on July 13, 1931, was ratified in France by the Law of April 6, 1933. The decree of June 30, 1933, classified, among other things, under the term *drugs:* "Preparations made directly from the coca leaf and containing more than 0.1 percent of cocaine."

The director of the Central Hospital Pharmacy at the time estimated in a 1934 article on the subject that, in light of new regulations, preparations of coca should now only be obtained "with coca from Bolivia containing 0.70 percent total alkaloids, soluble in ether," and that tincture of coca "should contain not less than 0.05 percent and no more than 0.07 percent of total alkaloids, soluble in ether." It concluded that, despite the new restrictions:

> The formula of coca wine would not be changed. However, it could bring the formula to 50 grams of leaves for 1,000 grams of wine. It

Cover of the pulp novel *Chez les trafiquants de cocaïne* ("Among the Cocaine Smugglers"), 1932 by Guy de Teramond.

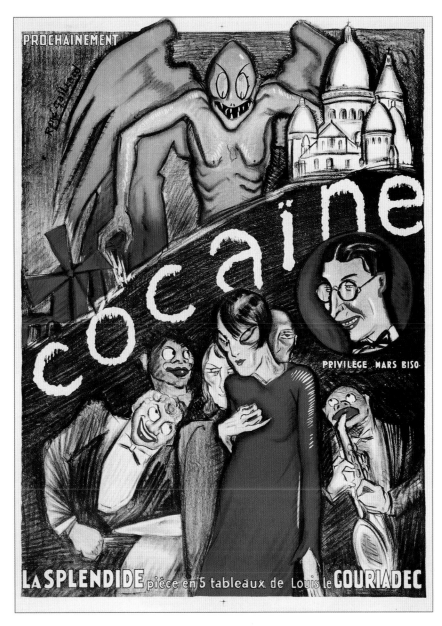

Poster by René Gaillard (?–1960) for Louis le Gouriadec's play *Cocaïne*, 1926. Courtesy of J. Santo Domingo.

would contain a maximum of 0.30 to 0.35 [percent] of alkaloids per liter. Under these conditions, the coca tincture and coca wine would not be subject to accounting requirements.[43]

If we are to believe the author of the article, the formula of Vin Mariani therefore would not need to be changed as a result of the decree.

Did the Mariani Company modify its preparations? It is likely, but we do not know precisely when. The *Vidal* pharmaceutical dictionary of

From Prescription
to Prohibition

Cover illustration by Spina
of the sheet music for
Cocaïne! ca. 1920.

Advertisement for
the Apéritif Mariani.

1946 listed Vin Tonique Mariani (sold in 1-liter and half-liter bottles) containing 16.65 grams of coca per liter of wine, compared with the 60 grams of the original formula per half liter.

A decree from the Ministry of Health on February 24, 1951, stated that coca-leaf preparations were exempt if they represented less than 6 percent of the total weight and less than 60 grams of the maximum weight of the substance publicly available. The coca-tincture preparations, which had only recently been classified in Table A, were exempt if they represented less than 60 percent of the total weight and less than 125 grams of the maximum weight of the substance publicly available. Coca wines were in the list of the exempted products.

The *Répertoire des spécialités pharmaceutiques* in 1954 still listed no less than twenty different coca wines, five concentrated extracts of coca, and twelve elixirs, half made with coca leaves and the rest with coca tincture, which contained fewer alkaloids. Among these products two came from the Mariani Company: the Tonique Mariani and the Terpine Mariani, a preparation to cure respiratory diseases based on turpentine and coca.[44]

The Last Years

After the death of Angelo Mariani on April 1, 1914, his son Jacques continued the work of his father. The pharmacy at 41, boulevard Haussmann was sold in 1930.[45] On the death of Jacques in 1935, his son, Angelo (1914–1978), took over the business. Coca-based products gradually disappeared from the catalog of the Mariani Company. There only remained the Elixir Mariani, which was still marketed in 1929, along with their flagship product, Vin Mariani, which was sold until 1954, when it changed its name to Tonique Mariani. It contained 120 grams of coca tincture and 66 grams of sugar per liter. It was found in pharmacies until 1963. Its therapeutic indications were for asthenia, convalescence, organic and nerve disabilities, neurasthenia, loss of appetite, and lymphatism. The Terpine Mariani, which contained 56 grams of coca tincture, 10 grams of terpine, 400 grams of alcohol, and 266 grams of sugar, disappeared in 1962. Over the years, an Apéritif Mariani, an Amer Mariani (bitters), and a Quina Mariani were introduced for the cafés and other licensed premises, apparently without much success.[46]

The company also marketed several other patent medicines such as Antimucose, Rectoquintyl, and Oxyuryl.

Photo of Mariani with the great poet Frédéric Mistral.

In 1958 the company was taken over by the Lelong laboratory. Both laboratories coexisted at the same address until 1960, when the Mariani Company ceased operation. Lelong marketed Vin Mariani until 1963. In 1973 they left the buildings at 10 rue de Chartres in Neuilly, the former

From Prescription
to Prohibition

headquarters of the Mariani Company. Lelong was bought in turn by the Synthelabo laboratory the following year. Shortly after, the plant and buildings built by Mariani were demolished.[47]

Thus ended the nearly century-long history of an extraordinary "pharmaceutical" product that in its time was probably, according to a contemporary American researcher, the most prescribed medicine in the world.[48]

Few products have aroused such enthusiasm, garnered such an abundance of comments and reviews, and benefited from such an exceptional and innovative promotional campaign.

Conclusion: Coca Today

Toward a Revival—the Bolivian Case

Recent Scientific Studies

The laws prohibiting trade and use of coca have not detracted from the renewed interest it has generated over the past few decades. These prohibitive measures, however, pose a real problem for the Andean countries that have maintained the habit of chewing coca leaves for centuries. For the indigenous populations of these countries, the use of coca is at once social, religious, medicinal, and even magical. It is used to treat many diseases and deficiencies: hunger, cold, fatigue, stomach pain, fever, headache due to altitude, respiratory infections, and psychiatric diseases.

Studies on the therapeutic value of coca leaf have multiplied. Botanists and doctors, mostly Americans, have published works on the subject. Among them is one published in 1975 at Harvard on the nutritional value of coca. It compared the composition of the coca leaf with fifty common foods in Latin America: fruits, vegetables, cereals, legumes, and nuts. The study showed that coca contains less fat than the average of the fifty foods, and has less vitamins B_1, B_3, and C. However, it has more calories, more carbohydrates, and more protein, fiber, calcium, iron, phosphorus, and vitamins A and B_2.[1]

In another study on the therapeutic value of coca in contemporary medicine published in 1981 in the *Journal of Ethnopharmacology,* Dr. Andrew Weil wrote that during his field research over several years, he has not seen:

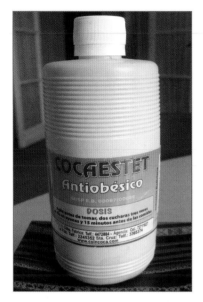

Coca-based slimming product.
Courtesy of the Bolivian Embassy
in France.

Coca-based antidiabetes product.
Courtesy of the Bolivian
Embassy in France.

Conclusion:
Coca Today

Any signs of physical deterioration attributable to the leaf. I have never seen an instance of coca toxicity. Nor have I observed physiological or psychological dependence on coca. Even life-long chewers seem able to get the effect they want from the same dose over time: there is no development of tolerance and certainly no withdrawal syndrome upon sudden discontinuance of use.

Based on his observations of regular consumers of coca, after reviewing the scientific literature on the issue, and based on his own clinical experience on 250 patients, he recommended the use of the coca leaf in the following cases:

1. In painful and spasmodic conditions of the entire gastrointestinal tract.
2. As a substitute stimulant for coffee in persons who consume much coffee and suffer exacerbations of gastrointestinal conditions from that drug.
3. As a fast-acting antidepressant.
4. As a treatment for acute motion sickness.
5. As adjunctive therapy in programs of weight reduction and physical fitness. Coca is anorexic and stimulating, unlike amphetamines, it provides some nutrients and does not produce toxicity or dependence.
6. As an energizer for persons engaged in heavy physical work, including certain athletes.
7. As symptomatic treatment of toothache and sores in the mouth.
8. As a laryngeal tonic in persons who must use their voices more than usual, such as professional singers and public speakers.
9. As a substitute stimulant to wean users of amphetamines and cocaine from those drugs.
10. As a normalizer of carbohydrate metabolism and treatment for hypoglycemia and diabetes mellitus.
11. As a tonic and normalizer of body functions.

For Dr. Weil, the most appropriate methods of administration would be lozenges or chewing gum.[2]

Between 1991 and 1995 the World Health Organization (WHO), in collaboration with the United Nations Interregional Crime and Justice

Coca Toothpaste.
Courtesy of
Ronald K. Siegel.

Research Institute (UNICRI), undertook the largest research ever conducted on coca and cocaine. Forty-five researchers from seventeen countries, including professors from five U.S. universities, gathered data, analyzed scientific journals, and interviewed hundreds of users and scientists in twenty-two cities in nineteen developed or developing countries.

The report concluded that the traditional uses of coca had no adverse health effects and played a positive role in the therapeutic, sacred, and social domains among the indigenous people of the Andean region. The report also noted that it played an important role in the subsistence economy of the village communities in these countries.

In March 1995, the WHO issued a press release announcing the publication of this report. At the general meeting of the organization the following May, the representative of the United States, upset by the forthcoming release of this report, denounced its conclusions for being too favorable to coca. He added that his country would stop funding the organization if it did not disavow this report. The secretariat of the WHO tried to defend the objectivity and rigor with which this report had been conducted. It was all in vain; the report was never published.[3]

A clinical study conducted in 1997 by the ethnopharmacologist Michel Sauvain, with some forty farmers of the Altiplano, both coca consumers and not, showed that:

> Chewing the leaves does not contribute to an increase in the physical capacities of the chewers, on the other hand, it allows them to sustain a prolonged effort and stimulates their respiratory system. This effect on endurance was observed only among regular users of coca and not among casual users. This greater stamina in physical effort is attributed to better blood circulation, to an action on catecholamines (chemical mediators of the nervous system), and to an increase in the number of red blood cells, which promote greater

Conclusion:
Coca Today

185

muscle oxygenation. Moreover, it was observed that the traditional consumption of coca leaves, considered by some as a food substitute, does not cause a decrease in appetite.[4]

Coca Policy:
The Bolivian Example

It is estimated that in Bolivia about three million people consume coca, which is 36 percent of the population. Annual consumption amounts to 20,000 tons, with a total production of 36,000 tons.[5]

In 2006, Bolivia elected the former leader of the coca growers union, Evo Morales, as president of the republic. His motto was *Coca si, cocaina no* (Coca yes, cocaine no). Section 384 of the new Bolivian constitution stipulates that the country "protect the original and ancestral Coca recognized as a cultural heritage and a renewable natural resource of Bolivia's biodiversity."

Coca elixir and liqueur. Courtesy of the Bolivian Embassy in France.

The area devoted to the cultivation of coca in Bolivia amounted to 27,500 hectares in 2006; 28,900 hectares in 2007; 30,500 in 2008; 30,900 in 2009; and 31,000 hectares in 2010. Since 2011, the area planted has decreased each year, reaching 23,000 hectares in 2013. According to the report of the United Nations Office against Drugs and Crime (UNODC), the net reduction of coca cultivation in the area

Conclusion:
Coca Today

Coca Boliviana placard.

Watercolor, pencil, Indian ink by Hugo d'Alesi (1849–1906). Courtesy of J. Santo Domingo

between 2010 and 2013 was 28 percent. Of the 23,000 hectares, 12,000 are considered as legal for traditional uses such as chewing, medicine, and religious rituals. In 2017 Bolivia's authorities passed a bill to increase the land area allotted to legal cultivation of the coca crop from 12,000 hectares to 22,000. The total value of the production of coca leaves in 2012 was $332 million, or 1.2 percent of gross domestic product (GDP) and 13 percent of agricultural GDP.

In 2009, Bolivia destroyed about 6,500 hectares of illegal plantations. In 2012, 11,000 hectares and four tons of cocaine were destroyed. In 2017, the figures were, according UNODC, 3.3 tons of cocaine hydrochloride and 13.7 tons of cocaine base. Bolivia, which tries to preserve traditional culture in addressing the trade in cocaine, spends more than $20 million in the fight against drug trafficking. In addition, it has invested $5 million in the *Coca si, Cocaina no* program to promote the use of coca for legal consumption (coca infusions, medicinal applications, energy drinks, and so on). In 2010, the United States still ranked Bolivia among the "bad students" in the fight against drugs, possibly in response to the expulsion of the American antidrug agency, the Drug Enforcement Administration (DEA), by President Morales in 2009.

Today, Bolivia produces and markets many products made from coca: flour, candies, jams, teas, cosmetics and pharmaceuticals, soft drinks, and, of course, liqueurs and wines.

Conclusion: Coca Today

Coca liqueur.

Coca ointment. Courtesy of the
Bolivian Embassy in France.

Coca wine.

Coca soda. Courtesy of the
Bolivian Embassy
in France.

In 2009 the Bolivian government invested $1.7 million in the construction of a packaging plant for the marketing of products derived from the coca leaf near Cochabamba, in the Chapare region. "After the third year of production we will be able to penetrate foreign markets, i.e., in 2014 or 2015," said the General Directorate of Marketing and Industrialization of Coca (Digcoin), which is under the deputy minister of Coca and Integral Development. Potential markets were initially selling a decocainized product to neighboring Latin American countries. Five years later, the plant is abandoned and has not produced anything for months.

Conclusion:
Coca Today

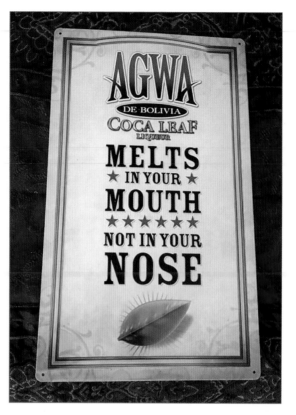

Agwa de Bolivia coca liqueur.

A packing plant for coca-derived products, located in La Paz, was inaugurated in August 2013 by President Evo Morales. The plant processes 213 tons of coca leaves yearly, producing preparations of coca-leaf and stevia combined with medicinal plants.

In March 2009, President Morales went to Vienna to the headquarters of the United Nations Commission on Narcotic Drugs. During his speech, he took some coca leaves out of his pocket and started chewing them, explaining that he has consumed coca for ten years, which did not prevent him from becoming the president of Bolivia and working eighteen hours a day. He called for the removal of paragraphs 1 and 2 of Article 49 of the 1961 Vienna Convention on Narcotic Drugs, which lists coca leaves among narcotic substances. The article states that the consumption of coca should disappear within twenty-five years.

In 2011, Bolivia was the first country to withdraw from the Vienna Convention on Narcotic Drugs. Morales said that his country will rejoin the convention only if the article banning the chewing of coca leaves is repealed. In January 2013, Bolivia formally reinstated the convention, which added a specific clause allowing its people to continue chewing coca leaves. Reinstatement was possible only if a third or more of the 183 member states did not object. According to a spokesman for the UN, only fifteen of them did, including France, the United States, the United Kingdom, Italy, Canada, Germany, and Russia.

On March 11, 2013, in a speech in Vienna at the headquarters of the United Nations Commission on Narcotic Drugs, President Morales recalled the existence of a tonic made from coca leaves in nineteenth century Europe, known by the name of Vin Mariani, which was very popular and appreciated, even by Pope Leo XIII. "I hope that the new pope, who will be elected soon, will resume the use of Vin Mariani," said the Bolivian president.

It seemed that the wishes of the Bolivian president would be fulfilled when, in December 2016, the Irish company Babco Europe proudly announced the release—153 years after the original—of a new Vin Mariani. The company noted that they intend to replicate the historical recipe as closely as possible. "Using a combination of pharmaceutical reports from the early 1900s and pharmacopeia journals, over a period of 10 years working with world master blenders, leading pharmacologists and flavorologists, we were able to piece together the original Vin Mariani recipe." With a difference of course: the coca leaves used are decocainized.

The CEO of Babco Europe, Mark Wilson, describes his Vin Mariani as "rich dark ruby red in colour, with deep lush honeyed fruit flavours, racy acidity and an earthy aroma that has an elegant, powerful and smooth finish."

Only time will tell if it will be as successful as its illustrious predecessor.

Conclusion:
Coca Today

Photography of Mariani by Nadar.

Notable Praise for Mariani and His Work

....

Supplementary Testimonials

Note: In the following, the source *A. M.* stands for *Albums Mariani*.

Pope Benedict XV: "The Holy Father wishes that the weakened in health always find in the properties of your firm's tonic, a principle of vigor and strength" (*A. M.,* vol. 14).

Léon Bloy, writer: "Received a case of Vin Mariani. . . . The Gods are thirsty, me too" (1 November 1903, *Journal inédit,* vol. 3, Paris: L'âge d'homme, 2007 p. 253).

Edouard Branly, physicist: "Vin Mariani must be one of the rare agents that slow the aging of our cells. Confident of this, and owing to its agreeable taste, I have eagerly adopted it" (*A. M.,* vol. 9).

Savorgnan de Brazza, explorer: "The excellent Vin Mariani is very popular throughout the Congo. Therefore the powers who signed the Berlin Act should have protected the freedom of trade of Vin Mariani against any monopoly" (*A. M.,* vol. 5).

Louis de Broglie, Nobel Prize in Physics: "Physics can really be a very difficult science . . . physicists must drink a lot of Vin Mariani" (*Supplément illustré,* 1930).

Sketch by Umberto Brunelleschi (1879–1949) in *Supplément illustré*, 1930

Sketch by Hubert-Denis Etcheverry (1867–1950), in *Albums Mariani*, vol. 9.

Colette, writer: "A glass of Mariani, or two, or three . . . One feels like a faun without it!" (*A. M.,* vol. 14).

Thomas Edison, scientist: "Mr. Mariani, I take pleasure in sending you one of my photographs for publication in your Album" (*A. M.,* vol. 2).

Camille Flammarion, scientist: "Rays of sunshine in a bottle, while eminent artists savor you as gastronomes, I salute you as an astronomer, O Vin Mariani, long live the sun" (*A. M.,* vol. 3).

Notable Praise for
Mariani and His Work

Advertising drawing
by Henri Delaspre
(1868–1918).

Loïe Fuller, dancer: "My kingdom for a Shakespeare head, a Molière tongue, a Dumas pen to praise our Mariani! It is not wine, it is sustenance for the home of the soul! Let us then all learn not its abuse, but its use. . . ." (*A. M.,* vol. 5).

Léon Gaumont, pioneer of the motion picture industry: "The problem of the talking movie has not been solved soon enough to allow to present, as if he is alive, Angelo Mariani, the creator of the famous wine that bears his name" (*Supplément illustré*, 1929).

Dr. G. Gilles de La Tourette, neurologist: "With all my thanks to Mr. Mariani whose wonderful wine is a powerful tonic for all neurasthenics" (*A. M.,* vol. 6).

Charles Gounod, composer: "To my dear friend A. Mariani, beneficent discoverer of that admirable Peruvian coca wine, which has so often restored my strength" (*A. M.,* vol. 1).

José Maria de Heredia, poet: "Peru, land of gold where Manco-Cápac reigned, you have produced nothing more valuable than coca" (*A. M.,* vol. 3).

Sketch by Ferdinand Bac (1859–1952), in *Albums Mariani*, vol. 9.

Notable Praise for Mariani and His Work

Grand Rabbi Zadoc Kahn: "I had read much praise of Vin Mariani in prose and in poetry, and I was a little skeptical. With a rare kindness, you allowed me to judge for myself; my conversion is complete. Honor to Vin Mariani" (*A. M.,* vol. 4).

General Lyautey: "All my sympathy for Vin Mariani, as with anything that gives life, strength, courage" (*A. M.,* vol. 13).

Louise Michel, anarchist: "Vin Mariani has something of the will, it doubles one's energy" (*A. M.,* vol. 10).

Drawing by Henry Detouche (1854–1913).

Mounet-Sully, actor: "As long one drinks it, he sings, laughs, vibrates, loves. He dreams about the future, of glory, of infinity! Nothing is better than vin Mariani except Mariani himself" (*A. M.,* vol. 1).

Henri Poincaré, mathematician: "20 Mariani = 100 T" [a pun in French: "100 T" = "cent-T" = *santé* = "health"] (*A. M.,* vol. 12).

Drawing, 1909, by Evert van Muyden (1853–1922).

Henri de Régnier, writer: "To Mr. Mariani, by whom our happy era has tasted your benefits, O Coca!" (*A. M.,* vol. 5).

Jules Renard, writer: "Before drinking Mariani wine and appearing in this album, I was wondering, with some concern, if I wasn't sick and if I had any talent. But now I feel reassured" (*A. M.,* vol. 9).

Jean Richepin, writer: "When will come she to whom no male / Never knew how to say nay / May her nose at my last gasp / Smell your wine, Mariani" (*Supplément illustré,* 1908).

Edmond Rostand, writer: "Mariani, your wine is digestive, comforting and tonic. . . . I always keep a flask on my work table" (*A. M.,* vol. 4).

Gaston Saint-Pierre, painter: "Had Mohammed known Vin Mariani, he certainly would not have forbidden it" (*A. M.,* vol. 5).

Notable Praise for
Mariani and His Work

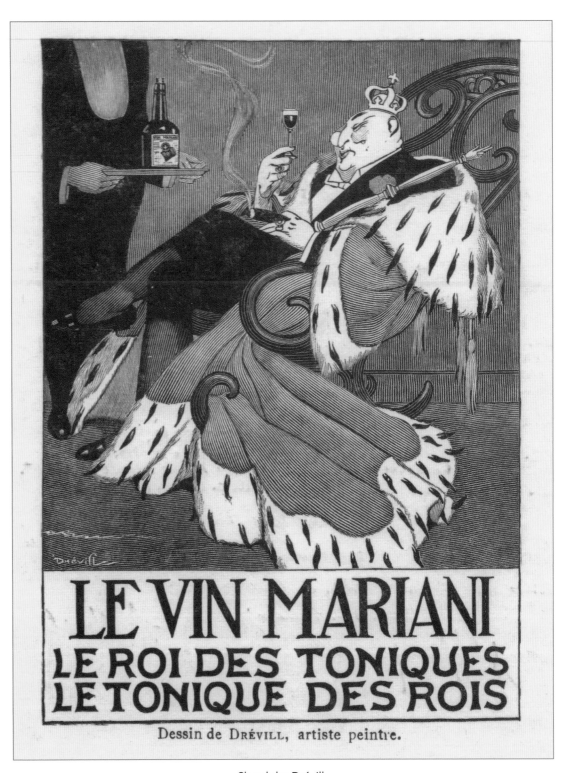

Sketch by Drévill,
in *Supplément illustré*, 1920.

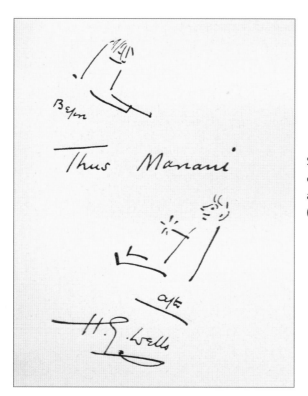

Sketch by H. G. Wells, writer, of himself before (depressed) and after drinking Vin Mariani (radiant). (*A. M.*, vol. 12).

Paul Valéry, writer: "As the role of the mind developed, man no longer found only in food for the body enough to support this particular [mental] energy. He searched everywhere—compounds, drugs, philters, elixirs, potions. Finally Mariani appeared" (*Supplément illustré,* 1927).

Dr. Fernand Widal, physician: "To popularize, as Mr. Mariani has done, a medicine as precious as coca, is to render a great service to therapeutics" (*A. M.,* vol. 7).

Chronology of Coca

6050 BCE Radiocarbon analysis of coca leaves found in the Nanchoc Valley in Peru indicates that coca chewing dates back to this era.

2000 BCE Containers of lime from the Valdivia culture (discovered during excavations in Ecuador) indicate coca use.

1499 The Dominican Tomás Ortiz is the first to mention the existence of coca.

1535 Historian Gonzalo Fernández de Oviedo is the first to describe the physiological effects of coca.

1562 and **1568** Ecclesiatical Councils are held in Lima, where the issue of coca is debated. Prohibitionists and antiprohibitionists debate each other.

1567 It is estimated that 2,000 Spaniards (8 percent of the European population in Peru), are involved in the coca trade, and that 300,000 Indian adults use coca, nearly 20 percent of the population.

1569 The king of Spain, in an edict, rejects the idea of prohibition, arguing that coca mitigates the severity of the working conditions for native Peruvians.

1574 The doctor and botanist Nicolas Monardes is the first to describe the psychoactive properties of coca leaves.

1605 The magistrate Claude Duret, in a botany book, makes the first detailed mention of coca in French.

1653 The Jesuit Bernabé Cobo mentions that toothache can be relieved by chewing coca leaves.

Depuis que le VIN MARIANI, au temple de la Coca, entrevu jadis dans les forêts vierges du Pérou par les lointains Conquistadors, et réédifié à Paris, coule en vraie fontaine de Jouvence, le Marianisme est devenu comme une religion qui a pour adeptes fervents :

Souverains, rois et reines, savants fatigués par les grands travaux de la pensée, prélats, lettrés et artistes, reines du monde et reines du théâtre, orateurs, magistrats, soldats et explorateurs débilités, femmes anémiées, enfants, tous les malades et les convalescents, les neurasthéniques et les influenzés, les délicats comme aussi les robustes et les bien portants.

Illustration by Albert Robida (1848–1926) in *La Vie Parisienne*, December 13, 1902.

1662 The first mention of coca in literature appears in a poem entitled "The Legend of Coca," written by an English poet who was passionate about botany, Abraham Cowley.

1749 The botanist Joseph de Jussieu sends some samples of coca to the Museum of Natural History in Paris to be examined by the botanist Carl Linnaeus and then by the botanist Jean-Baptiste Lamarck.

Chronology of Coca

Mariani bust by Théodore Rivière (1857–1912) Courtesy of E. Mariani.

1786 Lamarck classifies the plant in the family *Erythroxylaceae* under the name *Erythroxylon coca.*

1838 Angelo Mariani is born.

1859 Italian physician and anthropologist Paolo Mantegazza publishes the first article on coca.

1859 The German chemist Albert Niemann isolates an alkaloid that he names *cocaine* from an extract of coca leaves.

1862 The first mention of a coca wine is made in the medical thesis of Louis Gustave Demarle.

1863 The first references to coca preparations are made by Dr. Reis and pharmacist Joseph Bain.

1865–1869 In France, Angelo Mariani creates Vin Mariani à la Coca du Pérou.

1870 Mariani publishes a brochure on Quinquina Mariani.

1873 Mariani moves his pharmacy to 41 boulevard Haussmann in Paris.

1878 Mariani publishes the pamphlet "La Coca du Pérou et le vin Mariani."

1880 Mariani will be, indirectly, at the origin of the discovery of the anesthetic properties of the main alkaloid of coca, cocaine, by Dr. Coupard—and this before the work of Koller.

1880 Mariani opens a branch of his company in New York.

1880 Appearance of the journal *The Therapeutic Gazette* by Parke Davis Laboratories in Detroit. Twenty articles on coca will be published in this journal between 1880 and 1884.

1880 In New York, the Liebig Company launches Coca Beef Tonic.

1884 Sigmund Freud publishes his first article on coca and cocaine, "Über Coca."

1884 The Austrian ophthalmologist Karl Koller, discovers the anesthetic action of cocaine.

Advertising sketch by Yves Barret, in *La Vie parisienne*, March 19, 1881.

1884 Dr. John S. Pemberton, pharmacist in Atlanta, creates his French Wine Coca whose formula was clearly copied from Vin Mariani.

1885 Mariani moves his laboratory to 10–12 rue de Chartres in Neuilly-sur-Seine.

Illustration by Léon Lebegue (1863–1944) in *Pervenche*, 1900.

1885 Mariani publishes his study "La coca et la cocaïne."

1885 Vin Mariani and Mariani Tea are administered to U.S. president Grant, who is suffering from throat cancer, to allow him to finish writing his memoirs. After this, Mariani and his products became very famous in the United States.

1886 Pemberton, following the passage of the law prohibiting alcohol in Atlanta, replaces the wine in his drink with sugar syrup, citric acid, and caffeine mixed with soda. He calls the drink Coca-Cola.

1887 Oregon is the first state to ban the sale and possession of cocaine without a prescription.

1888 Mariani issues a study on *Coca and Its Therapeutic Applications* that will be published in the United States.

1888 Publication of the first volume of the *Tales of Angelo Mariani* collection, *Le Cas du vidame* by L. Beaumont, illustrated by Robida. The thirteenth and last volume will appear in 1904.

1891 The first booklet with twenty-four testimonials and portraits is published under the title *Album Mariani*.

1893 *Supplément illustré* is first published in the newspaper *Le Figaro*.

1894 The first *Album Mariani* volume is published.

1894 Jules Chéret draws the famous poster for Vin Mariani.

1894 The Food Commission of the state of Ohio ranks Vin Mariani in a list of adulterated products, questioning the amount of coca leaves it contains. The commission loses at trial, and Vin Mariani is allowed again.

1900 Mariani publishes a first series of sixty promotional postcards with drawings of Vin Mariani that first appeared in the *Albums*.

1901 Dr. William G. Mortimer publishes an important study called *Peru: History of Coca, "the Divine Plant" of the Incas.*

1902 Mariani creates a quarterly magazine in New York called *Mariani's Coca Leaf* (1902–1906), which is distributed free to some 50,000 doctors.

1902 The American Pharmaceutical Association estimates there are some 200,000 cocaine users in the United States.

Illustration by Léon Lebegue (1863–1944) in *Pervenche*, 1900.

1903 Coca-Cola begins to decocainize coca leaves, which are still used in the formula today.

1903 The analyses carried out by the state Board of Health of Pennsylvania on Vin Mariani to determine if it contained cocaine show that its presence is "incidental to its manufacture and not intentional . . . and too small to lead to the suspicion of cocaine."

1906 The 10-million-bottles-sold mark for Vin Mariani is reached.

Chronology
of Coca

1906 President Roosevelt signs the Pure Food and Drug Act. Patent medicines must include the list of their ingredients on the labels of their products.

1906 The American Council on Pharmacy and Chemistry examines samples of Vin Mariani. According to its report, the Mariani Company is unclear about the origin of the product and made misleading statements about its therapeutic value.

1907 The Massachusetts State Board of Health publishes in its annual report a list of preparations containing cocaine. Among these products, twenty-one were coca wines, including Vin Mariani.

1907 The Mariani Company informs the public that its product is now completely free of cocaine.

1909–1912 Mariani publishes a second set of 150 advertising postcards.

1912 It is estimated that more than 50 percent of the prostitutes in Montmartre are cocaine addicts.

1914 Angelo Mariani dies at his home in Valescure, on the French Riviera.

1914 The Harrison Narcotic Tax Act requires, among other things, that those who produce preparations of coca leaves keep a register of sales. This does not apply to decocainized preparations.

1916 Promulgation of the law in France on toxic substances. (In the law, drugs are listed in Table B.)

1924 According to questionable police figures, there are no less than 80,000 cocaine addicts in Paris alone!

1925 The fourteenth and final volume of *Album Mariani* is published.

1925 The International Convention on Narcotic Drugs is signed in Geneva.

1930 The decree implemented by the Convention adds coca leaves as well as coca preparations, including coca wine, that contain more than 0.10 percent cocaine to Table B.

1930 The Mariani pharmacy at 41 boulevard Haussmann is sold.

A bust of Mariani by Jean Baffier (1851–1920). Courtesy of the Centre artistique Jean Baffier.

1931 A new International Convention on Narcotic Drugs is signed in Geneva.

1932 *Supplément illustré* is published for the last time.

1933 Mariani Company's offices in New York close.

1946 The Vin Tonique Mariani contains 16.65 grams of coca per 1 liter of wine.

Angelo Mariani
1838–1914

ANGELO MARIANI

LE PROPAGATEUR DE LA COCA

1838 - 1914

1954 The *Répertoire des spécialités pharmaceutiques* lists no fewer than twenty different coca wines. Among them, Tonique Mariani, which replaces Vin Mariani, and contains 120 grams of tincture of coca.

1958 The Mariani Company is taken over by Lelong laboratory. Both laboratories coexist until 1960, the year that marks the disappearance of the Mariani Company.

1961 The Single Convention on Narcotic Drugs is signed in New York. It asks in particular for the total eradication, in the following twenty-five years, of all the coca plantations in Bolivia and Peru.

LE VIN MARIANI

CHŒUR DES AMANTS. — Vin Mariani, liqueur divine ! Donne-nous la jeunesse éternelle, avec l'amour robuste qui, dans la vie console, encourage et sourit !

CHŒUR DES ÉPOUX. — Bon Vin Mariani, vin des ménages heureux ! Donne-nous, avec la joie de vivre, de beaux enfants auxquels, quand nous aurons des cheveux blancs, nous dirons : « Soyez reconnaissants à la Coca ! »

CHŒUR DES VIEILLARDS (dans la coulisse). — Ah ! si vieillesse pouvait... Enfin le Vin Mariani nous reste encore !

Lucien Métivet (1863–1932) in *La Vie Parisienne*, February 21, 1903.

1963 The production of Tonique Mariani is halted.

1975 Harvard publishes a major study on the nutritional value of coca.

1981 A major study on the therapeutic value of coca is published in the *Journal of Ethnopharmacology*.

2006 Bolivia elects the former leader of the coca-growers union, Evo Morales, as president.

2011 Bolivia is the first country to withdraw from the Convention on Narcotic Drugs of 1961.

2013 Bolivia formally reinstates the Convention when it adds a specific clause allowing the Bolivian people to continue chewing coca leaves.

2013 Bolivian president Evo Morales, in his speech at the headquarters of the Commission on Narcotic Drugs of the United Nations in Vienna, recalls the existence in nineteenth-century Europe of Vin Mariani.

2016 A new Vin Mariani is launched by the Irish company Babco Europe.

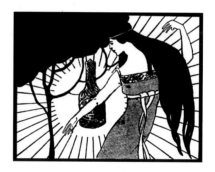

Notes

CHAPTER 1.
A BRIEF HISTORY OF COCA

1. T. D. Dillehay, J. Rossen, D. Ugent, et al., "Early Holocene Coca Chewing in Northern Peru," *Antiquity* 84, no. 326, (2010): 939–53; Timothy Plowman, "The Identification of Coca (*Erythroxylum* species): 1860–1910," *Botanical Journal of the Linnaean Society,* 84 (1982): 329–53; T. Plowman, "Coca Chewing and the Botanical Origins of Coca (*Erythroxylum* spp.) in South America," in *Coca and Cocaine: Effects on People and Policy in Latin America,* ed. Deborah Pacini and Christine Franquemont (Cambridge, MA: Cultural Survival, 1986) 5–33. For a good synthesis on the botanical and the geographical aspects of coca see the unpublished thesis by Jyri Soininen, "Industrial Geographies of Cocaine," University of Helsinki, Faculty of Science, Department of Geography 2008, 19–24.

2. Donald W. Lathrap, *El Ecuador antiguo: Cultura, ceramica y creatividad 3000–300 AC* (Chicago: Field Museum of Natural History 1976).

3. Frederic Engel, "Early Sites on the Peruvian Coast," *Southwestern Journal of Anthropology* 13 (1957): 54–68, and idem, "A Preceramic Settlement on the Central Coast of Peru: Asia Unit I," *Transactions of the American Philosophical Society* 53, part 3 (1963); C. A. Hastorf, "Archaeological Evidence of Coca (Erythroxylum coca, Erthroxylaceae) in the Upper Mantaro Valley, Peru," *Economic Botany* 42 (1987): 292–301; Olive Griffiths, "Examination of Coca Leaves Found in a pre-Inca Grave," *Quarterly Journal of Pharmacy and Pharmacology* (1930): 52–58; Mario A. Rivera et al., "Antiquity of Coca-Leaf Chewing in the South Central Andes: A 3,000-year Archaeological Record of Coca-Leaf Chewing from Northern Chile," *Journal of Psychoactive Drugs* 37, no. 4 (2005): 455–58.

4. Joseph Kennedy, *Coca Exotica: The Illustrated Story of Cocaine* (Rutherford, NJ: Fairleigh Dickinson University Press, and New York: Cornwall Books, 1985), 25–26.

5. Amerigo Vespucci, *First Four Voyages of Amerigo Vespucci* (London: B. Quaritch, 1893), 28–9. Originally published as *Lettera di Amerigo Vespucci delle isole nuovamente trovate in quattro suoi viaggi* (Florence: Gian Stefano, 1505), 20.

6. Gonzalo Fernández de Oviedo, *La Historia general de las Indias* (Seville: J. Cromberger, 1535), book. 6, chap. 20.

7. Vicente Valverde, "Carta del Obispo del Cuzco al Emperador sobre asuntos de su Iglesia y otros de la Gobernación de aquel país, Cuzco, 20 de marzo de 1539," in *Colección de documentos Inéditos relativos al descubrimiento, conquista y colonizacion de las Posesiones Españolas en América,* ed. J. F. Pacheco (Madrid 1865), 3:98.

8. Pedro Cieza de León, *The Incas of Pedro de Cieza de León* (Norman, Oklahoma: University of Oklahoma Press, 1959), 352. Originally published as *La Crónica del Perú* (Seville: Martin de Montesdoca, 1553), chap. 96.

9. Agustin de Zarate, *Historia del descubrimiento y conquista del Peru* (Antwerp: M. Nucio, 1555), book 1, chap. 8, p. 15.

10. Juan de Matienzo, *Gobierno del Perù* [1567] (Buenos Aires: Compañia Sud-Americana de Billetes de Banco, 1910), 90.

11. See Juan de Matienzo, and Joseph Gagliano, *Coca Prohibition in Peru: The Historical Debates* (Tucson: University of Arizona Press, 1994), 33–34.

12. Nicolas Monardes, *Joyfull newes out of the newe founde worlde . . .* (London: E. Allde, 1596), 102. Originally published as *Historia medicinal que trata de las cosas que se traen de nuestras Indias Occidentales que sirven al uso de medicina* (Seville: A. Escrivano, 1574), 114–15.

13. José de Acosta, *Natural and Moral History of the East and West Indies* (1604), 273. Originally published as *Historia natural y moral de las Indias* (Seville: J. de Leon, 1590), book 4, chap. 22, pp. 252–53.

14. Claude Duret, *Histoire admirable des plantes et herbes esmerveillables et miraculeuses en nature* (Paris: N. Buon, 1605), 195–200.

15. Garcilaso de La Vega, *El Inca: Royal Commentaries of the Incas.* 2 vols. (Austin, Tex.: University of Texas Press, 1966), 509. Originally published as *Primera parte de los Commentarios reales, que tratan del origen de los Yncas, reyes que fueron del Peru . . .* (Lisbon: Pedro Crasbeeck, 1609), book 8, chap. 15, p. 212.

16. Bernabé Cobo, *Historia del Nuevo Mundo,* manuscipt, Lima, Peru, 1653, book 5, chap. 29.

17. Abraham Cowley, *Plantarum libri duo* (London: Flesher, 1662).

18. Herman Boerhaave, *Institutiones medicae in usum annuae exercitationis* (Leyden: J. van der Linden, 1708), §68.

19. For a detailed description of the amazing adventure of Joseph de Jussieu, see Patrick Drevet, *Le corps du monde* (Paris: Seuil, 1997), and Jean-Marie Pelt, *La cannelle et le panda: Les naturalistes explorateurs autour du monde* (Paris: Fayard, 1999), 83–92; Jean-Baptiste de Lamarck, *Encyclopédique méthodique. Botanique* (Paris: Panckoucke, 1786), 2:389–93.

20. Antonio Julián, *La Perla de la América, Observada y Expuesta en Discursos Históricos* (Madrid: A. de Sancha, 1787), 24–25, 34–35.

21. Paolo Mantegazza in *The Coca Leaf and Cocaine Papers,* Andrews & Salomon (eds.), (London: Harcourt Brace Jovanovich, 1975), 41. Originally published as "Sulle virtù igieniche e medicinali della coca, e sugli alimenti nervosi in generale," *Annali Universali di Medicina* (March 1859), 492–93. See also Giuliano Dall'Olio, "Paolo Mantegazza: Memoria sulle proprietà terapeutiche della coca," *La Rivista Italiana della Medicina di Laboratorio,* no. 7 (2011):

228–39, and Antonio Aimi, "Mantegazza e la coca: una ricerca de rivalutare," in *Paolo Mantegazza e l'evoluzionismo in Italia,* ed. C. Chiarelli and W. Pasini (Florence: Firenze University Press, 2010), 163–75.

22. Sigmund Freud, *Cocaine Papers* (New York: Stonehill, 1974), 53. It is the first of four articles that Freud would devote to coca and to cocaine between 1884 and 1887. Originally published as "Über Coca," *Centralblatt für die gesamte Therapie,* vol. 2 (1884), 289–314, it was partially translated in *The Saint Louis Medical and Surgical Journal* vol. 47 (December 1884), 502–5.

23. Albert Niemann, "Über eibe neue organische Base in den Cocablättern," *Archiv der Pharmazie* 153, no. 2 (1860): 129–256.

24. On the history of coca see also William G. Mortimer, *Peru: History of Coca, "the Divine Plant" of the Incas* (New York: J. H. Vail, 1901), 148–176; Kennedy, *Coca Exotica,* 15–58; Gagliano, *Coca Prohibition,* 25–75; Soininen, "Industrial Geographies of Cocaine," 55–64.

CHAPTER 2.
ANGELO MARIANI, FATHER OF COCA WINE

1. G. Davenay, "Les obsèques de M. Mariani," *Le Figaro,* April 7, 1914, 3–4; and "Angelo Mariani," *Simple revue,* April 15, 1914, 227–28.

2. "Angelo Mariani et la presse," *Simple revue,* May 1, 1914, 260–61.

3. "Angelo Mariani et la presse," *Simple revue,* May 1, 1914, 259–60.

4. René Lara, "Angelo Mariani," *Le Figaro,* April 2, 1914, 3.

5. Jean-Ange Galletti, *Histoire illustrée de la Corse* (Paris: Imprimerie de Pillet Fils, 1863), 568.

6. *Notice sur le Quinquina Mariani précédée d'un aperçu sur l'histoire et les propriétés du quinquina* (Paris: Maillard-Bossuat, 1870). The brochure is signed by M. Mariani, chemist's assistant in Bastia. The previous year Mariani also published a four-page brochure in Spanish, *Extracto Mariani hidro-alcoolico de quina* (1869), which tells us that he was selling his preparation in Paris and in Mexico.

7. Mariani himself varies on the precise date of its creation. In his study *La coca et la cocaïne,* (Paris, 1885), he wrote: "From 1867, when we started our first publicity trials, in France and in Europe, on coca preparations . . ." In the booklet *Coca Erythroxylon (Vin Mariani): Its Uses in the Treatment of Diseases* (New York, 4th ed. 1886), published by the Mariani Company, 1863 is mentioned on p. 53 as the date of creation. Dr. William G. Mortimer, in his seminal book, *Peru: History of Coca,* wrote: "In 1865, Dr. Fauvel, of Paris, used a preparation of coca which had been prepared for him by Mariani" (412). This date was confirmed by Dr. Fauvel himself in a letter to the editor published in the *New York Medical Journal* of December 31, 1887: "Vin Mariani, which, since 1865, I have had occasion to prescribe daily in my clinic, as well as in private practice . . ." (748). But Fauvel later contradicts himself, fixing the date at 1870 in a letter to Mariani dated May 1, 1890, when he writes: "20 years ago . . . we made known to the astonished medical world the virtues of a plant that it had never heard of. Its odd name coca . . . is now on everyone's lips." *Figures contemporaines* vol. 1, 1894.

8. Georges Régnal, "Angelo Mariani," *Nouvelle Revue,* May 15, 1914, 211.

9. On the use of coca by Dr. Fauvel, see Freud, "Über Coca," 314; the notice "Dr. Fauvel," *Album Mariani* vol. 1 (Paris: Flammarion 1894); Charles Fauvel, "De l'anesthésie produite par le chlorhydrate de cocaïne sur la muqueuse pharyngée et laryngée," *Gazette des hôpitaux,* no. 134 (November 20, 1884): 1067; Dr. P. Collin, "De la coca et ses véritables propriétés thérapeutiques," *L'Union médicale,* August 11, 1877, 240; Dr. Scaglia, "La coca et ses applications thérapeutiques," *Gazette des hôpitaux* (May 10–12, 1877), 428.

10. Régnal, "Angelo Mariani," 213–14. René Lara, in his obituary in *Le Figaro,* April 2, 1914, mentions, "one of the most illustrious members of the Comédie Française" that Mariani cured successfully for problems of depression and fatigue caused by her career as an artist.

11. "Atonie musculaire laryngée traitée avec succès par le vin de coca," *L'Union médicale,* December 4, 1875, 842–43.

12. Dr. Gazeau, "Observations d'emploi du coca," *Revue de thérapeutique médico-chirurgicale,* October 15, 1872, 540–41.

13. Georges Claretie, "Figures contemporaines," *Le Figaro,* March 3, 1906, 1.

14. Louis Gustave Demarle, "Essai sur la Coca (Erythroxilon Coca) du Pérou" medical thesis, Paris, 1862, 45. Before Demarle's thesis, the first study on coca published in France, in 1853, is the one by Dr. Hugues-Algernon Weddell, *Notice sur la coca, sa culture, sa préparation, son emploi et ses propriétés* (Paris: Impr. de Mme. Vve. Bouchard-Huzard, 1853).

15. Dr. Reis, "Action physiologique de la coca: Son emploi en thérapeutique," *Journal des connaissances médicales pratiques,* January 20, 1863, 19–23, and *Bulletin général de thérapeutique* (April 1866): 175–77; Freud, "Über Coca."

16. Joseph Bain, *Vin tonique nutritif de Joseph Bain à la quinquina et à la coca combinés.* This four-page brochure doesn't have any publication date (the stamp of the registration of copyright of the French National Library indicates 1863); see also *De la coca du Pérou et de ses préparations* (Paris: Asselin, 1867), reissued in 1869, 1870, and 1875.

17. Chevrier, *Notice sur les propriétés et l'usage du coca du Pérou: Vin et élixir de coca* (Paris: F. Malteste, 1867), reissued in 1869.

18. Angelo Mariani, "La coca du Pérou," *Revue de thérapeutique médico-chirurgicale,* 1872, 148–52 and *Le Monde pharmaceutique,* February, 20, 1875, 25–26.

19. André Néde, "Fortuna . . .", *Le Figaro,* February 7, 1914, 1.

20. Régnal, "Angelo Mariani," 214–15.

21. From the *Journal de jurisprudence commerciale et maritime,* 1888, 172–77, as well as from the *Journal des tribunaux de commerce,* 1888, 270–74, we learn that by a judgment of the Commercial Court of Paris on September 25, 1886, Mariani was turned down in his request for the dissolution of the company after the death of his partner, arguing that the heirs of the deceased were minors. Being ordered to pay the costs, he appealed. On April 7, 1887, the Court of Appeal of Paris confirmed the judgment and declared that there was no need to dissolve the company.

22. See the notice "Dr. Coupard," in *Album Mariani,* vol. 7 (Paris: Floury, 1902).

Notes

It should be noted that the father of American laryngology, Dr. Louis Elsberg, declared having received and used for his operations, cocaine hydrochloride that had been provided to him by Mariani in 1884. See Hermann Knapp, *Cocaine and Its Use in Ophthalmic and General Surgery* (New York: Putnam, 1885), 59, and Dr. William Oliver Moore, "The Physiological and Therapeutical Effects of the Coca Leaf and Its Alkaloid," *New York Medical Journal,* January 3, 1885, 20.

23. Dr. Laborde, "Note préliminaire sur l'action physiologique de la cocaïne et de ses sels," *Comptes rendus hebdomadaires des séances et mémoires de la Société de biologie,* November, 22, 1884, 631–38.

24. *Lancet,* January 3, 1885, 43.

25. Paul Reclus, *L'anesthésie localisée par la cocaïne* (Paris: Masson, 1903), 3.

CHAPTER 3.
MARIANI'S LABORATORY
AND ITS COCA-BASED PRODUCTS

1. Émile Gautier, "La coca considérée au point de vue scientifique et au point de vue industriel," *La science française,* June 24, 1898, 321–24.

2. Régnal, "Angelo Mariani," 225–26.

3. Neuilly-sur-Seine, Conseil general, *État des communes à la fin du XIXe siècle, publié sous les auspices du Conseil général. Neuilly-sur-Seine. Notice historique et renseignements administratifs* (Montévrain: Impr. de l'école d'Alembert, 1904), 180–81.

4. Mortimer, *Peru: History of Coca,* 179; *Mariani's Coca Leaf,* December 1903, 60.

5. G. Davenay, "Le dixième tome de Mariani," *Le Figaro,* June 12, 1906, 2.

6. *État des communes à la fin du XIXe siècle,* 180.

7. *Simple revue,* April 1, 1917, 829.

8. Gautier, "La coca considérée," 321–24.

9. Mortimer, *Peru: History of Coca,* 178.

10. Gautier, "La coca considérée," 321–24.

11. Angelo Mariani, *Coca and Its Therapeutic Application* (New York: J. N. Jaros, 1892), 50.

12. Mortimer, *Peru: History of Coca,* 178.

13. Mariani, "La coca du Pérou," *Le Monde pharmaceutique,* February 20, 1875, 25–26; *Mariani's Coca Leaf,* March 1904, 108; Joseph Uzanne, "Une innovation dans la publicité," *La publicité moderne,* no. 8 (August 1907), 11; and *État des communes à la fin du XIXe siècle,* 181. Concerning the geographical origin of the French coca imports we could cite the German scientist Theodor Walger who writes that: "Exports of Bolivian coca leaves to Europe were small and largely confined to France"; See also *Die Coca, ihre Geschichte, geographische Verbreitung und wirtschaftliche Bedeutung* (Berlin: Druck von E. S. Mittler und Sohn, 1917), translation in Steven B. Karch, *A History of Cocaine: The Mystery of Coca Java and the Kew Plant* (London: Royal Society of Medicine, 2003), 151. Emma Reens in her pharmacy thesis of 1919 wrote that: "Bolivia sends only small quantities to Europe and especially to Le Havre. The imports

in France were 40 tons in 1911," *La Coca de Java: Monographie historique, botanique, chimique et pharmacologique* (Lons-le-Saunier: L. Declume, 1919), 17–18. At the same time it should be noted that France imported 55 tons of coca leaves from Peru; see A. W. K. de Jong, "Het cocavraagstuk," in *Teysmannia* 23 (1912), 674. In 1912 this amount drops to 25.8 tons and 9.4 in 1913; See also *Handelsberichten* (The Hague: Ministerie van landbouw, nijverheid en handel, 1914), 326–27. The American researcher Paul Gootenberg considers that Mariani used only coca leaves of Bolivian origin; See *Andean Cocaine: The Making of a Global Drug* (Chapel Hill: University of North Carolina Press, 2008), 25, 45, 57, 65, 112, 115.

14. Mariani, "La coca du Pérou," 25–26.
15. "Coca Wines of the Market," *Druggists' Circular and Chemical Gazette,* February 1886, 32; *Mariani's Coca Leaf,* October 1903, 27–28; and the *Journal of the American Medical Association (J.A.M.A.),* November 26, 1906, 1751. These alcohol levels are confirmed by the examination of a bottle of Vin Mariani with magnetic resonance imaging (MRI) performed by Professor Massimo Marcone at the University of Guelph in Ontario, Canada, in October 2011. See http://atguelph .uoguelph.ca/2011/10/food-scientists-analyze-1895-vintage-bordeaux.
16. *Simple revue,* May 15, 1901, 298.
17. *La Couturière,* October 1, 1901, 219–20.
18. *Simple revue,* April 15, 1908, 243.
19. *Simple revue,* July 1, 1896, 206.
20. Dr. Lelong, *La coca du Pérou et ses applications thérapeutiques* (Paris: Clavel, 1883), 97.
21. Davenay, "Le dixième tome de Mariani," 2.
22. *État des communes à la fin du XIXᵉ siècle,* 181; another source indicates that in 1895, "more than 500,000 bottles of Vin Mariani were sold in England and America," see Emile Zola, *Correspondance, Octobre 1893–Septembre 1897,* vol. 8 (Montreal: Presses de l'Université de Montreal, and Paris: Éditions du C.N.R.S., 1991), 280, note 1.
23. Mariani, "La coca du Pérou," 25–26; Mariani, *Coca and Its Therapeutic Application,* 50–62; *La coca du Pérou et le Vin Mariani* (Paris: Mariani & Co., 1878) 17–19; *Mariani's Coca Leaf,* November 1904, and also Lelong, *La coca du Pérou et ses applications thérapeutiques,* 151.
24. Leader, "Les champions du sport et le vin Mariani," *La vie au grand air,* supplement, May 21, 1899.
25. Lelong, *La coca du Pérou et ses applications thérapeutiques,* 93.

CHAPTER 4.
THE MEDICINAL VIRTUES OF VIN MARIANI

1. *American Druggist,* July 1885, 39.
2. *Supplément illustré,* published in *Journal des débats politiques et littéraires,* March 30, 1897, 3–4.
3. Mariani, *Coca and Its Therapeutic Application,* 62; See also Marc Laffont, "Erythroxylon Coca: Its Value as a Medicament," *New York Medical Journal,*

December 7, 1889, 629; Mariani, *Coca Erythroxylon (Vin Mariani),* 3; *Le Figaro*, April 25, 1885, 3, mentions Vin Mariani. One of the physicians of President Grant, Dr. George F. Shrady, mentions in his article "The Surgical and Pathological Aspects of General Grant's Case," in *The Medical Record,* August 1, 1885, 121–24, that he administered coca and cocaine to his illustrious patient. The article "General Grant's Condition," *Medical Record,* March 7, 1885, 268, mentions that he was given "fluid extract of coca."

4. Mariani, *Coca and Its Therapeutic Application,* 69–78.

5. Leonard Corning, *Brain Exhaustion with Some Preliminary Considerations on Cerebral Dynamics* (New York: D. Appleton, 1884), 78, 212; Cyrus Edson, *La Grippe and Its Treatment: For General Readers* (New York: D. Appleton, 1891), 39; Beverley Robinson, "Heart Strain and Weak Heart," *Medical Record,* February 26, 1887, 238; Charles. E. Sajous, "Coca in Hoarseness of Professional Singers," *J.A.M.A.,* May 3, 1890, 25.

6. Mark Twain, *What Is Man? and Other Philosophical Writings,* ed. Paul Baender. (Berkeley: University of California Press, 1973), 459.

7. John F. Maisch, "On Coca Leaves," *The Medical and Surgical Reporter,* August 3, 1861, 399–400; Isaac Ott, "Physiological Action of the Leaves of the Erythroxilon Coca on the Excretion of Urine," *Medical Times,* November 15, 1870, 56–57.

8. *Coca Erythroxylon and Its Derivatives: A Résumé of Their History, Botanical Origin, Production and Cultivation, Chemical Composition, Therapeutic Application, Physiological Action, and Medicinal Preparations* (Detroit: Parke, Davis & Co., 1885), 4. In 1880, in a previous pamphlet, Parke, Davis already had in its catalogue certain coca specialties. See *An Epitome of the Newer Materia Medica, Standard Medicinal Products, and Fine Pharmaceutical Specialties* (Detroit: Parke, Davis & Co., 1880), 16, 52.

9. W. H. Bentley, "Erythroxylon Coca in the Opium and Alcohol Habit," *Therapeutic Gazette,* September 1880, 253–54; E. C. Huse, "Coca Erythroxylon, a New Cure for the Opium Habit," *Therapeutic Gazette,* 1880, 256–57; A. F. Stimmel, "Coca in the Opium and Alcohol Habits," *Therapeutic Gazette,* April 15 and August 1881, 132–33 and 252–53.

10. William S. Searle, *A New Form of Nervous Disease: Together with an Essay on Erythroxylon Coca* (New York: Fords, Howard and Hulbert, 1881), 90, 125, 134, 138.

11. Louis Lewis, letter to the editor, *Lancet,* April 1, 1876, 520.

12. F. E. Stewart, "Coca-leaf Cigars and Cigarettes," *Philadelphia Medical Times,* September 19, 1885, 933–5.

13. Joseph F. Spillane, *Cocaine: From Medical Marvel to Modern Menace in the United States, 1884–1920,* (Baltimore: The John Hopkins University Press, 2000), 61.

14. Mortimer, *Peru: History of Coca,* 491–516.

15. Angelo Mariani, *Figures contemporaines,* vol. 7 (Paris: Floury, 1902).

16. *Simple Revue,* March 15, 1900, 176

17. Mariani, *Coca and Its Therapeutic Application,* 54–55.

18. Mariani, *Coca and Its Therapeutic Application,* 55–56.

Notes

19. Gazeau, "Observations d'emploi du coca," 540.

20. Scaglia, "La coca et ses applications thérapeutiques," 428.

21. Dr. Nitard, "Des toniques locaux et des toniques diffusibles," *Gazette des hôpitaux,* November 29, 1877, 1100.

22. Collin, "De la coca et ses véritables propriétés thérapeutiques," 239; Freud, "Über Coca."

23. Odin, "Des propriétés toniques et stimulantes de la coca," *France médicale,* 1884, 1738.

24. *Simple revue,* December 15, 1901, 641, and *Le Magasin colonial et du voyage,* November 15, 1901.

25. *Le Figaro,* October 16, 1909, 1.

26. André Néde, "Envois de France," *Le Figaro,* March 10, 1913, 1.

27. Paul Léautaud, *Journal littéraire—Tome IV (1922–1924),* May 22, 1922 (Paris: Mercure de France, 1957), 37.

28. Fernand Gregh, *L'Âge de fer* (Paris: Grasset, 1956), 35.

CHAPTER 5.
THE FATHER OF MODERN ADVERTISING

1. Marcel Bleustein-Blanchet, *La rage de convaincre* (Paris: R. Laffont, 1970), 43.

2. See William H. Helfand, *Quack, Quack, Quack: The Sellers of Nostrums in Prints, Posters, Ephemera, and Books* (New York: Grolier Club, 2002); James Harvey Young, *The Medical Messiahs: A Social History of Health Quackery in Twentieth-Century America* (Princeton, NJ: Princeton University Press, 1967).

3. *The Edinburgh Review,* February 1843, 6; See also E. S. Turner, *The Shocking History of Advertising* (London: Michael Joseph, 1953), 91.

4. Turner, *Shocking History,* 205, 209.

5. Philip Kotler et al., *Marketing Management* (Harlow, UK: Pearson Education, 2009), 479–80.

6. Régnal, "Angelo Mariani," 210.

7. Ververt, "Les Treize . . .", *Le Figaro,* January 20, 1911, 1; Francis Trépardon, "Charles Gounod compose un hymne pour le Vin Mariani" *Revue d'histoire de la pharmacie,* no. 338 (2003): 313–15; Jean-Rémy Julien, *Musique et publicité: du cri de Paris aux messages publicitaires radiophoniques et télévisés* (Paris: Flammarion, 1989), 147–56.

8. Marie Bonaparte, *À la mémoire des disparus,* vol. 2, *L'Appel des sèves* (Paris: P.U.F., 1958), 853–54.

9. Mortimer, *Peru: History of Coca,* 180.

10. http://www.societe-perillos.com/mariani_2.html (site discontinued).

11. René Lara, "Le miracle de la plante," *Le Figaro,* February 9, 1912, 1.

12. Octave Uzanne, "Un don à la Bibliothèque Nationale," *Le Figaro,* November 25, 1909, 2.

13. Octave Uzanne, "Prélude iconographique," in Angelo Mariani, *Figures contemporaines,* vol. 1 (Paris: Flammarion, 1894), 4.

14. Jules Claretie, "Préface," Angelo Mariani, *Figures contemporaines,* vol. 4 (Paris: Floury, 1899).

15. *Gazette des tribunaux,* December 10, 1898, 1135; December 17, 1898, 1159; January 21, 1899, 71; Armant Bigeon, "L'affaire Reutlinger contre Mariani," *Bulletin du photo-club,* 1899, 1–9 and 33–40. For the testimonials in favor of Mariani, see E. Ratoin, "La reproduction des photographies," *Le Monde artiste,* October 8, 1899, 652–53.

16. O. Uzanne, "Un don à la Bibliothèque Nationale," 2–3.

17. Letter of November 27, 1902 (vol. 3, 1); *Le Figaro,* November 25, 1909, 3.

18. Letter in vol 9, 1, and *Le Figaro,* June 29, 1910, 1, and *Simple Revue,* July 15, 1910, 431.

19. Letter in vol 4, 2. For some other examples of erotic testimonials and for a psychoanalytic study of the content of the *Albums Mariani* see Pierre Eyguesier, *Comment Freud devint drogman* (Paris: Navarin Éditeur, 1983), 104–7 and 75–78; 95–116; 153–56.

20. See Patrick Avrane, *Drogues et alcool: Un regard psychanalytique* (Paris: Campagne Première, 2007), 57–99, for an interesting psychoanalytic study of the content of the *Albums Mariani,* and Franziska Blaser, "La poésie dans les *Albums Mariani,* paper from the conference *Les Poètes et la publicité, Actes des Journées d'études des 15 et 16 janvier 2016,* Université Sorbonne Nouvelle-Paris 3, 2017, 20–32, on the use of poetry in the testimonials.

21. Jules Arren, *La publicité lucrative et raisonnée, son rôle dans les affaires* (Paris: Bibliothèque des ouvrages pratiques, 1909), 366; see also Joseph Uzanne, "Une innovation dans la publicité," *La publicité moderne,* no. 8 (August 1907): 8–11.

22. L. de Beaumont, *Le Cas du Vidame,* (Paris: Librairie illustrée, 1888), 39.

23. Jules Claretie, *Un chapitre inédit de Don Quichotte* (Paris: H. Floury, 1898), 26–27.

24. See on this subject Guy Devaux, "Le Vin Mariani et sa publicité: Un intéressant recueil de Contes," *Revue d'histoire de la pharmacie,* no. 325 (2000): 131–32; Pierre Julien, "Les Contes à Mariani," *Revue d'histoire de la pharmacie,* no. 328 (2000), 522–24, and "Angelo Mariani et son vin de coca: Mécénat et publicité," *Fermacia e industrializacion* (Madrid: Homenaje al doctor Guillermo Folch Jou, 1985), 130–34; Helfand, *Quack, Quack, Quack,* 140–43; Jean-Claude Viche, "Les Contes à Mariani écrits ou illustrés par Robida," *Le Téléphonoscope* (Bulletin des amis d'Albert Robida), no. 19 (November 2012): 25–32. See the list of the tales in bibliography.

25. See on the subject, Alain Delpirou, "Mariani et les cartes postales," *Le vieux papier,* July 2005, 314–18. It contains mistakes on the dates and the number of the postcards printed.

26. The medals and plates were engraved by Oscar Roty (1846–1911), Pierre-Charles Lenoir (1879–1953), Louis-Eugène Mouchon (1843–1914), Louis Patriarche (1872–1955), Victor Peter (1840–1918), and Georges Dupré (1869–1909). On this topic see David Hill, "Art of Promotion: Mariani Medals at the ANS," *ANS Magazine,* no. 3 (2016): 40–51.

27. George Sand, *La Bonne Déesse de la pauvreté. Ballade* (Paris: Angelo Mariani, 1906); Jules Claretie, *Deux visions* (Paris: Angelo Mariani, 1910); Louis Vossion, *Trois femmes pour un époux: Conte birman* (Paris: Angelo Mariani, 1910).

CHAPTER 6.
THE HOST OF ALL HOSTS

1. *Simple Revue,* June 1, 1902, 275–76

2. Émile Berr, "Un déjeuner de vernissage," *Le Figaro,* April 30, 1914, 1; see also Régnal, "Angelo Mariani," 227, 228.

3. *Simple revue,* June 1, 1912, 302.

4. Sandrine Doré, "Un artiste à la table d'Angelo Mariani, menus et publicités illustrés par Robida," *Le Téléphonoscope* (Bulletin des amis d'Albert Robida), no. 14 (October 2007): 16–19; Léon Maillard, *Les Menus et programmes illustrés, invitations, billets de faire part, cartes d'adresse, petites estampes, du XVIIe siècle jusqu'à nos jours* (Paris: G. Boudet, 1898), 253–57.

5. *Simple revue,* May 1893, 217; El. Antillano "Le Pérou à Paris," *La revue diplomatique,* April 11, 1891, 9–10.

6. D. Langer, "La villa Marie," *Simple revue,* September 1, 1910, 515.

7. F. Scott Fitzgerald, "How to Live on Practically Nothing a Year," *Saturday Evening Post,* September 20, 1924.

8. Emilie Michaud-Jeannin, "La nymphe de la Fontaine," *Var Matin,* September 2, 1990.

9. D. Langer, "La villa Andréa (villa Mariani)," *Simple revue,* May 1, 1910, 258–61.

10. Pierre Fernez, "Mariani à Valescure . . . il y a 100 ans," *Courrier de Valescure,* no. 23 (March 1996): 6–9.

11. Bonaparte, *À la mémoire des disparus,* 853–54.

12. Emilie Michaud-Jeannin, "Villa Andréa: Le souvenir d'Angelo Mariani," and "Villa Mariani, beauté architecturale anéantie," *Var Matin,* August 8, 1989, and November 6, 1990.

CHAPTER 7.
THE TIME OF ORDEALS: THE IMITATORS

1. Émile Gautier, "Le triomphe du Vin Mariani," *Le Figaro,* October 27, 1903, 3.

2. *Therapeutic Gazette,* September 15, 1881, 351.

3. See in particular Eugène Carmouche, *Dictionnaire médical et thérapeutique des spécialités pharmaceutiques et médicinales* (Paris: Carmouche, 1885); M. Gautier and F. Renault, *Formulaire des spécialités pharmaceutiques composition, indications thérapeutiques, mode d'emploi et doses* (Paris: J.-B. Baillière, 1895); Gautier and Renault, *Nouveau formulaire des spécialités pharmaceutiques* (Paris: J.-B. Baillière, 1901); Dr. Vincent Gardette, *Formulaire des spécialités pharmaceutiques* (Paris: J.-B. Baillière et fils, 1907) 6 editions until 1912; Dr. Roger Hyvert, *Description, emploi et valeur en clientèle des traitements nouveaux: médicaments, médications et formules, spécialités pharmaceutiques* (Paris: Maloine, 1912).

4. *Notice sur le vin Bravais* (Paris, 1890); *Le Vin Bravais à l'Exposition de 1900* (Paris: Vin Bravais, 1900).

5. Pierre Julien, "A propos de publicité pharmaceutique," *Revue d'histoire de la pharmacie,* no. 255 (December 1982): 270–71, and idem, "Huile de foie de

morue et Vin Désiles, ou un médicament au théâtre," *Revue d'histoire de la pharmacie,* no. 274 (November 1987): 221–23; C. Raynal and T. Lefebvre, "Alexandre Choffé et le vin Désiles," *Revue d'histoire de la pharmacie,* no. 330 (2001): 193–214, et "Les deux vins Désiles," *Revue d'histoire de la pharmacie,* no. 338 (2003): 316–17.

6. *Le Figaro, Supplément illustré,* November 30, 1895, 2.

7. Among the other coca wines we can mention the names of Vin du Dr. Legendre, Quintonine, Vin du Dr. Clément, Vin cocainé pepsique, Vin fortifiant Bourdou, Vin fortifiant Cooper, Tonique Herdy, Vin Margaret, Vin Guislain à la coca du Pérou, Vin de viande composé, Quina-Coca Chaumel, Moto-Koca, Vin de Gloria, Vin du Dr. Rogé, Tonique Chapès, Quinquina Coca, Le Suprême coca, Vin Séguier, Vin et élixir de coca Debrest, Kola-Coca Barbin, Vin St. Hilaire, Élixir de Roussy, Vin Pipault, Korso, Vin Écalle, Cérébrine, Élixir et Tridigestif Gigon, Élixir Grez, Élixir vital Quentin, Liqueur Hor, Vin d'Auryan, Vin antidiabétique Rabot, Vin de coca iodé de Renaud, Vin de Franc, Vin de Gourou, Vin Moisan, Vin et Élixir Pausodun, Vin des trois toniques, Vin de Voguet, Tonique Cartaz, Vin Delanoë, Vin Auguet, Élixir Hampton, Vin Garde, Élixir de coca Vigier, Vin Bardy, Vin tonique du Dr. E. Abeille, Pélagine Fournier, Élixir Bertrand, Vin Duvallet, Vin de Barbarin, Pepsine Blanchard, Vin de Bastide, Vin Kalders, Vin de Fièvet, Solution du Dr. Watelet, Vin Brunot, Tonique Fougerat, Vin Duvallet, Biophorine, Vin de coca Detray, Vin Dupray, Vin tonique Lepère, Vin Saint-Germain, Vin du Dr. Jhames, Vin tonique Barbier, Vin oxygéné Panchèvre, Samo-vital, Vin tonique Mynusal, Vin tri-tonique et Vin de viande Aubéry, Coca Maurice, Vin tonique reconstituant Boisramé, Vin Souverain, etc.

8. "The Composition of Some Proprietary Food Preparations: II Tonic Wines," *British Medical Journal,* May 29, 1909, 1307, and Mr. Homan, "Medicated Cheer," *Pharmaceutical Journal,* December 20, 2003, 867–68.

9. On the company, see *La coca: I suoi usi e le sue proprietà* (Bologna: Gio. Buton, 1876). On Jane Atché, see Claudine Dhotel-Velliet, *Jane Atché* (Lille, France: Le Pont du Nord, 2009).

10. Spillane, *Cocaine,* 79–84. The *Druggists Circular* price list in April, 1903, lists twenty-seven coca-wine products.

11. *Atlanta Constitution,* June 8, 1884.

12. "A Wonderful Medicine," *Atlanta Journal,* March 10, 1885, 4. See on the topic, Monroe Martin King, "Dr. John. S. Pemberton: Originator of Coca-Cola," *Pharmacy in History* 29, no. 2 (1987): 85–89, as well as the best book on the subject, Mark Pendergrast's *For God, Country and Coca-Cola: The Definitive History of the Great American Soft Drink and the Company That Makes It,* 3rd ed. (New York: Basic Books, 2013).

13. "Wonderful Coca," *Atlanta Constitution,* June 21, 1885.

14. *Atlanta Constitution,* November 17, 1886, 3.

15. *Atlanta Journal,* March 14 and 18, 1885.

16. *Atlanta Constitution,* June 28, 1885, 9.

17. Pendergrast, *For God, Country and Coca-Cola,* 34.

18. *New England Druggist,* 1899, 248–49.

19. See list in Pendergrast, *For God, Country and Coca–Cola,* 104.

20. Mariani, *Coca Erythroxylon (Vin Mariani): Its Uses in the Treatment of Diseases,* 1.

21. William Oliver Moore, "Rival Preparations of Coca," *New York Medical Journal,* October 24, 1885, 467.

22. Letter by William Oliver Moore in *New York Medical Journal*, October 24, 1885, 464.

23. Letter to the editor published in the *New York Medical Journal,* December 31, 1887, 748.

24. *Gazette du Palais,* part 2, 1905, 216–17.

25. "Vin Mariani Sustained by the Court," *Mariani's Coca Leaf,* November 1905, 17–18.

26. *Bulletin annexe au Journal officiel de la République française,* February 2, 1909, and Mariani, *Figures contemporaines,* vol. 12 (Paris: Floury, 1910). See also Thierry Lefebvre, "Mariani versus Mariani," *Revue d'histoire de la pharmacie,* no. 332 (2001): 545–47, and Cécile Raynal, "Mariani versus Mariani: Jugement et rebondissement," *Revue d'histoire de la pharmacie,* (2005): 100–101; Mariani, *Figures contemporaines,* vol. 11 (Paris: Floury, 1908).

CHAPTER 8.
FROM PRESCRIPTION TO PROHIBITION

1 Isaac Ott, "Cocain, Veratria and Gelsemium," in *Toxicological Studies* (Philadephia: Lindsay and Blakiston, 1874); and idem, "Coca and Its Alkaloid Cocain," *Medical Record,* 1876, 586.

2. "Cocaine's Terrible Effect: A Chicago Physician Becomes Insane from Using the Drug," *New York Times,* November 30, 1885, 1.

3. Howard Merkel, *An Anatomy of Addiction: Sigmund Freud, William Halsted, and the Miracle Drug Cocaine* (New York: Pantheon Books, 2011), 54–58.

4. On the use of cocaine in U.S. medical practice see Spillane, *Cocaine,* 14–42.

5. T. D. Crothers, "Cocaine-inebriety," *Quarterly Journal of Inebriety* 20, (1898): 370.

6. See, among other articles, "The Cocaine Habit among Negroes," *British Medical Journal,* November 29, 1902, 1729; Dr. Edward H. Williams, "Negro Cocaine 'Fiends' Are a New Southern Menace," *New York Times,* February 8, 1914, 12; "Cocaine Sniffers: Use of the Drug Increasing among Negroes of the South," *New York Daily Tribune,* June 21, 1903, 11.

7. "Cocaine in the United States," *Canadian Pharmaceutical Journal,* 42, 1909, 396. Quoted by Joseph Spillane, "Making a Modern Drug: the Manufacture, Sale, and Control of Cocaine in the United States, 1880–1920," in *Cocaine Global Histories,* ed. Paul Gootenberg, (New York: Routledge, 1999), 30.

8. Among the other movies are *The Curse of Cocaine* (1909); Romaine Fielding, *His Blind Power,* which was also known as *The Cocaine Fiend* (1913); Harry Meyers, *Cocaine Traffic* (1914); Herman Liebe, *Dope* (1914); John Noble, *Black Fear* (1915); Edwin August, *Bondwomen* (1915); George Fitzmaurice,

Big Jim Garrity (1916); Chester Withey, *The Devil's Needle* (1916); Frank Reicher, *Public Opinion* (1916); Allen Holubar, *Fear Not* (1917); Charley Chase [Charles Parrott], *Playmates* (1918); Chester Withey, *Her Honor, The Governor* (1926); Scott Pembroke, *Sisters of Eve* (1928); William O'Connor, *The Pace That Kills* (1928). On the topic of drugs, and notably, cocaine, in the American silent cinema, see Michael Starks, *Cocaine Fiends and Reefer Madness: An Illustrated History of Drugs in the Movies* (East Brunswick, NJ: Cornwall Books, 1982), 35–45; Kevin Brownlow, *Behind the Mask of Innocence: Sex, Violence, Prejudice, Crime: Films of Social Conscience in the Silent Era* (Berkeley: University of California Press, 1990), 96–119; Larry Langman, *American Film Cycles: The Silent Era* (Westport, CT: Greenwood Press, 1999), 200–210; Eric Schaefer, *"Bold! Daring! Shocking! True!" A History of Exploitation Films, 1919–1959* (Durham, NC: Duke University Press, 2001), 220–27.

9. Victoria Spivey recorded "Dope Head Blues" in 1927. Luke Jordan recorded "Cocaine Blues" the same year. This track was reissued in 1929 by the white singer Dick Justice under the title "Cocaine." Also in 1929, Charley Patton recorded "A Spoonful Blues," which speaks cryptically of cocaine addiction. In 1930 the Memphis Jug Band recorded "Cocaine Habit Blues." In 1934 Leadbelly recorded "Take a Whiff on Me." In 1938 Ella Fitzgerald sings "Wacky Dust" with the Chick Webb orchestra. Even the musical deals with the theme in the famous song by Cole Porter "I Get a Kick Out of You" in 1934. In 1936, the censors obtained the suppression of the verse about cocaine. See on the subject Harry Shapiro, *Waiting for the Man: The Story of Drugs and Popular Music* (London: Quartet Books, 1990), 22–24, and mainly Wolf R. Kempfer, *Die Cocaine Blues Story* (Löhrbach, Germany: Pieper and the Grüne Kraft, 2003).

10. Spillane, *Cocaine,* 65.

11. Annie Meyers, *Eight Years in Cocaine Hell* (Chicago: St. Luke Society, 1902), 11.

12. "Coca-Bola," *J.A.M.A.,* January 1, 1910, 63–64; "Tucker's Asthma Specific: An Insidiously Dangerous Cocain Mixture," *J.A.M.A.,* May 20, 1911, 1495–96; Daniel D. Gilbert, "The Cocaine Habit from Snuff," *Boston Medical and Surgical Journal,* February 3, 1898, 119. John Phillips Street in his book *The Composition of Certain Patent and Proprietary Medicines* (Chicago: American Medical Association, 1917) identifies three anti-asthma and fifteen anti-catarrh cocaine preparations. For a study of these various preparations see also L. F. Kebler, *Habit-Forming Agents: Their Indiscriminate Sale and Use a Menace to the Public Welfare* (Washington, DC: Government Printing Office, 1910), 10–12; and Spillane, *Cocaine,* 85–89 and 137–40.

13. Austin Flint, "The Effrontery of Proprietary Medicine Advertisers," *Medical News,* May 3, 1890, 488–89; Mariani & Co. "A Reply," *Medical News,* June 14, 1890, 663; and Mariani's *The Effrontery of Proprietary Medicine Advertisers* (New York: Mariani & Co., 1890). It should be noted that a favorable endorsement by Dr. H. Flint was published in the second edition of *The Efficacy of Coca Erythroxylon: Notes and Comments by Prominent Physicians* (Paris and New York: Mariani & Co., 1889).

14. *An Error of the Ohio Pure Food Commission* (New York: Mariani & Co., 1895). See also the articles published on this case in the *New York Times,* October 18, 25, and 28, 1894; "The Ohio Pure Food Law and Vin Mariani," *New York Medical Journal,* January 5, 1895, 31.

15. *Report and Official Opinions of the Attorney General of Pennsylvania* (Harrisburg, PA: W. M. Stanley Ray Pub., 1905), 294–95.

16. *Mariani's Coca Leaf,* May 1905, 70–72.

17. *Mariani's Coca Leaf,* March 1905, 53.

18. James Harvey Young, *Pure Food: Securing the Federal Food and Drugs Act of 1906* (Princeton, NJ: Princeton University Press, 1989).

19. *The Propaganda for Reform in Proprietary Medicines* (Chicago: American Medical Association, 1908), 87.

20. Scaglia, "La coca et ses applications thérapeutiques," 428, and Nitard, "Des toniques locaux et des toniques diffusibles," 1100, mention that a bottle of wine contained the equivalent of 120 milligrams of cocaine. Dr. Charles Mitchell in his analysis speaks of 132 milligrams (see "Coca Wines of the Market," *Druggists' Circular and Chemical Gazette,* February 1886, 32). The *J.A.M.A.* of November 26, 1906, 1751, speaks of the equivalent of 125 milligrams. The Mariani Company publishes in 1903 the results of analyses made by a laboratory in Paris on March 24, 1900, that mentions 110 milligrams of alkaloids. The analysis carried out on September 24 of the same year by a laboratory in Berlin concluded that cocaine contained in a bottle of Vin Mariani "is not present in detectable amount" (see *Mariani's Coca Leaf,* October 1903, 27–28). We do not think, contrary to what is written by some American authors, that Vin Mariani for the U.S. market contained more cocaine than the one for France. In our opinion the differences in dosing are due to the normal variations between the various analyses and the leaves used. What was unknown at the time was that the mixture of cocaine and alcohol was metabolized by the liver to form cocaethylene. It was not until 1990 that a group of researchers from Yale discovered that alcohol strengthened and prolonged the effect of cocaine.

21. Approximate average chosen according to various studies. See notably Steven B. Karch, *A Brief History of Cocaine* (Boca Raton, FL: CRC Press, 1998), 27.

22. Mariani, *Coca and Its Therapeutic Application,* 50, and also *Mariani's Coca Leaf,* October 1903, 17–19, 21–22, 25–26, and idem, January 1904, 72–73.

23. "Vin Mariani Report by Council on Pharmacy and Chemistry—with Comments," *J.A.M.A.,* November 26, 1906, 1751–53.

24. *Collective Testimony of the Benefit and Virtue of the Famous French Tonic, Vin Mariani* (New York: Mariani & Co., 1910), 272.

25. *Thirty-Ninth Annual Report of the State Board of Health of Massachusetts* (Boston: Wright & Potter, 1908), 381–82.

26. William H. Helfand, "An Assay of Coca Wine: An Eyewitness Account," *Pharmacy in History* 30, no. 3 (1988): 156.

27. *J.A.M.A.,* May 7, 1910, 1559.

28. Spillane, *Cocaine,* 139–40.

29. John Phillips Street, *The Composition of Certain Patent and Proprietary Medicines.* This applies to: Ayer's Vita Nuova, Carnick's Coca Muscatel, Celerina, Claflin's Coca Wine, Coca Calisaya, Cocainized Pepsin Chinchona Bitters, Kola Cardinette, Lambert's Wine of Coca, Maltine with Coca Wine, Mattison's Coca Wine, Metcalf's Coca Wine, Nichol's Compound Kola Cordial, Nyal's Coca Wine, Parker's Tonic Wine, Pilsbury Coke Extract, Quina Laroche, Webster's Wine Coca Leaves.

30. Thomas Moréno y Maïz, "Recherches chimiques et physiologiques sur l'Erythoxilum coca du Pérou et la cocaïne," medical thesis, Paris, 1868; F. Jolyet, "Recherches sur l'action physiologique de la cocaïne" *Comptes rendus des séances et mémoires de la Société de biologie* 1867 (Paris: Baillière, 1869), 162.

31. Magnan and Saury, "Trois cas de cocaïnisme chronique," *Comptes rendus hebdomadaires des séances et mémoires de la Société de biologie* (Paris: Masson, 1889), 60–63.

32. Marcel Briand et Vinchon, "Les priseurs de cocaïne," *Bulletin de la Société clinique de Médecine Mentale,* November 1912, 272. Georges Guillain, in "L'intoxication par la cocaïne," *Journal médical français,* June 15, 1914, 237, mentions 50 percent of the prostitutes and those in homosexual circles.

33. "Paris Fears Growth of Cocaine Craze," *New York Times,* December 1, 1912, C1; See also on this topic of a new epidemic Maurice Courtois-Suffit and René Giroux, *La Cocaïne, étude d'hygiène sociale et de médecine légale* (Paris: Masson, 1918), and of V. Cyril and Dr. Berger, *La coco: Poison moderne* (Paris: Flammarion, 1924).

34. Courtois-Suffit and Giroux, *La Cocaïne,* 22

35. Among the major stories and novels by famous authors who mentioned cocaine in the twenties and thirties, we can cite these: from Francis Carco: *Verotchka l'étrangère* (1923); *Rue Pigalle* (1928); *Les vrais de vrai* (1928); *Images cachées* (1929); *Prisons de femmes* (1931); *La lumière noire* (1934); *La dernière chance* (1935); *Brumes* (1935); from Pierre Mac Orlan: *Aux lumières de Paris* (1925); *Marguerite de la nuit* (1926); *La danse macabre* (1927); *Images secrètes de Paris* (1928); *Masques sur mesure* (1937); from Philippe Soupault *Le nègre* (1927); from Joseph Kessel: *Nuits de Sibérie* (1928); *Le coup de grâce* (1931); *Nuits de Montmartre* (1932); *Bas-fonds* (1932); from René Crevel: *La mort difficile* (1926); *Êtes-vous fous?* (1929); from Robert Desnos: "Ode à Coco" in *Corps et biens* (1930); from Victor Margueritte: *La Garçonne* (1922); from Jean Cocteau: *Le grand écart* (1923). Marcel Proust mentions it in *Remembrance of Things Past* when the Viscountess de Saint Fiacre is described as having taken cocaine for three years. Pulp literature also takes up this theme.

36. Emma Liébel recorded "La coco" in 1914, which will be reissued by the great Fréhel with success in 1931. Fréhel had been for long a big cocaine fiend with a consumption of 15 grams per day. She would have introduced her lover of the time, Maurice Chevalier, to cocaine. According to her biographers, she amused her audience by passing a handkerchief through her nasal septum ravaged by the drug. Damia was also a fervent consumer. Emma Liébel recorded "La coco, la gueuse" ("Coco the Wench") in 1923 and "C'est la coco" ("It's Coco") in

1926. Germaine Lix recorded "Madame Coco," with lyrics by Francis Carco, in 1924. Gina Manes recorded this title in turn in 1933. Nitta-Jo recorded "Cocaïne" in 1932. The same year La Palma recorded "L'idole blanche" ("The White Idol"). As for the men, Georgel sang "Margot 'la Coco'" in 1914 and then denounces "Les marchands d'illusions" ("The Merchants of Illusion"), which he recorded in 1930. Fortugé sings "Rêve de coco" ("Cocaine Dream") in 1922 that Louis Fournier recorded in 1930. At least two silent movies mention cocaine: *Barrabas* by Louis Feuillade (1919), and *Faubourg Montmartre* by Charles Burguet (1924).

37. Courtois-Suffit and Giroux, *La Cocaïne,* 115, and idem, "Le trafic de la cocaïne d'après les documents judiciaires récents; son extension, sa répression insuffisante; moyens d'y remédier," *La Presse médicale,* July 29, 1922, 1254.

38. Cyril and Berger, *La coco: Poison moderne,* 129–30.

39. Cyril and Berger, *La coco: Poison moderne,* 14. Five years after, in 1929, according to another police source, the number has been reduced to 30,000. See Maryse Querlin, *Les Drogués* (Editions de France, 1929), 46.

40. Maurice Courtois-Suffit and René Giroux, "Le trafic de la cocaïne, d'après les documents judiciaires récents; son extension et sa répression insuffisante," *Bulletin de l'Académie de médecine,* June 21,1921, 721–23. On the American soldiers involved in cocaine trafficking see Walter Duranty "Soldiers Smuggle Cocaine to French," *New York Times,* June 24, 1921, 31. For a history of cocaine consumption in the years 1920–1930 see Christian Bachmann and Anne Coppel, *Le Dragon domestique: Deux siècles de relations étranges entre l'Occident et la drogue* (Paris: Albin Michel, 1989), 242–57, 293–95; Jean-Jacques Yvorel, *Les poisons de l'esprit: Drogues et drogués au XIX e siècle* (Paris: Quai Voltaire, 1992), 156–64; Emanuelle Retaillaud-Bajac, *Les paradis perdus: Drogues et usagers de drogues dans la France de l'entre-deux-guerres* (Rennes: Presses Universitaires de Rennes, 2009), 38–45.

41. E. Dufau and L. G. Toraude, "La question coca devant le décret du 20 mars 1930," Bulletin des sciences pharmacologiques, May 1931, 97–101.

42. Dufau and Toraude, "Historique et commentaire de l'arrêté du 7 juillet 1931," Bulletin des sciences pharmacologiques, July 1931, 157–58.

43. A. Goris, A. Chalmeta, and C. Chalmeta, "La coca et les décrets de 1930 et 1931," *Bulletin des sciences pharmacologiques,* November 1934, 577–90, and December 1934, 645–60. For a history of antinarcotics legislation see Igor Charras, "Genèse et évolution de la législation relative aux stupéfiants sous la Troisième République," *Déviance et société,* nos. 22–24 (1998): 367–87.

44. Répertoire des spécialités pharmaceutiques. Fascicule 4, Substances relevant des conventions internationales sur les stupéfiants et médicaments en renfermant (Paris: Imprimerie Nationale, 1954), 385–403.

45. See the *Supplément Illustré* (28e série) of 1930 where the address doesn't exist anymore.

46. *Revue des vins et liqueurs et des produits alimentaires pour l'exportation 1929,* 460.

47. L'indicateur Bijou (annuaire des commerçants de Neuilly-sur-Seine) for the years 1958 to 1975; Dictionnaire de spécialités pharmaceutiques Vidal (Paris: Office de vulgarisation pharmaceutique) for the years 1957 to 1973; Guide Rosenwald, for the years 1957 to 1973.

48. Wade Davis, *Explorations and Discoveries in the Amazon Rain Forest* (New York: Simon & Schuster, 1997), 414–15.

CONCLUSION.
COCA TODAY

1. James A. Duke, David Aulik, Timothy Plowman, "Nutrition Value of Coca," *Botanical Museum Leaflets, Harvard University* 24, no. 6 (October 31, 1975): 113–19.

2. Andrew T. Weil, "The Therapeutic Value of Coca in Contemporary Medicine," *Journal of Ethnopharmacology* 3 (1981): 367–76; see also Anthony Henman and Pien Metaal, "Coca and Nutrition," *Drugs & Conflict,* no. 17 (June 2009): 4–7.

3. "Coca Yes, Cocaine, No? Legal Options for the Coca Leaf," *Drugs & Conflict,* no. 13 (May 2006): 7–8.

4. Michel Sauvain and Mercedes Villena Cabrera, *Usos de la hoja de coca y salud pública* (La Paz: Instituto Boliviano de Biología de Altura, 1997).

5. Frédéric Faux, *Coca! Une enquête dans les Andes* (Arles: Actes Sud, 2015), 108–9, 261.

Bibliography of Published Works by and about Angelo Mariani

Chronological List of Books and Articles Written by Angelo Mariani

Extracto Mariani hidro-alcoolico de quina para preparar instantemente el vino de quina. Paris, 1869.

Notice sur le quinquina Mariani, précédée d'un Aperçu sur l'histoire et les propriétés du quinquina. Paris: Maillard-Bossuat, 1870.

La Coca du Pérou et le vin Mariani: Le plus agréable et le plus efficace des toniques et des stimulants. Botanique, historique, thérapeutique. Paris: Mariani & Co., 1878. English trans., *Mariani Wine of Erythroxylon coca. Le vin Mariani à la coca du Pérou. Botanique. Historique. Thérapeutique,* Paris and New York: Mariani & Co., 1880.

Coca Erythroxylon (Vin Mariani): Its Uses in the Treatment of Disease: With Notes and Comments by Prominent Physicians. Paris and New York: Mariani & Co., 2nd ed., 1884; 3rd ed., 1884; 4th ed., 1886. Reprint: Charleston, SC: Nabu Press.

La coca et la cocaïne. Paris: A. Delahaye et E. Lecrosnier, 1885.

La coca et ses applications thérapeutiques. Paris: Lecrosnier et Babé, 1888; 2nd ed. 1895; English trans., *Coca and Its Therapeutic Application.* New York: J. N. Jaros, 1890; 2nd ed., 1892; 3rd ed, 1896; Spanish transl., *Pioneros de la coca y la cocaína.* Valencia: Éd. El Peón espía, 2011.

The Efficacy of Coca Erythroxylon: Notes and Comments by Prominent Physicians. Paris and New York: Mariani & Co., 1888; 2nd ed., 1889.

The Effrontery of Proprietary Medicine Advertisers. New York: Mariani & Co., 1890.

Album Mariani: Portraits contemporains gravés à l'eau forte. Paris: G. Richard, 1891.

Portraits from Album Mariani. New York: Mariani & Co., 1893; reprint: Charleston, SC: Nabu Press, 2010.

Figures contemporaines, tirées de l'album Mariani. 14 vols. Paris: E. Flammarion, H. Floury, G. Richard, 1894–1925.

An Error of the Ohio Pure Food Commission: Respectfully Submitted to the Medical Profession. New York: Mariani & Co., 1895.

Contemporary Celebrities: From Album Mariani of Paris, France. New York: Mariani & Co., 1901.

Eminent Physicians: With Biographical Notes of Members of the Paris Academy of Medicine. Paris: Mariani & Co., 1902; 2nd ed, 1903; reprint, Whitefish, MT: Kessinger, 2009.

Quelques figures contemporaines tirées des Albums Mariani: Portraits, autographes, notices biographiques rédigées par Joseph Uzanne. Portraits gravés sur bois par MM. H. Brauer, Ch. Clément et D. Quesnel. Strasbourg: A. Kopp, 1907.

Collective Testimony of the Benefit and Virtue of the Famous French Tonic, Vin Mariani. New York: Mariani & Co., 1910.

Portraits tirés de l'Album Mariani. 5 vols. Paris: Mariani & Co., 1911.

Articles and Journals by Angelo Mariani

"La coca du Pérou." *Revue de thérapeutique médico-chirurgicale* (March 15, 1872): 148–52.

"La coca du Pérou." *Le Monde pharmaceutique* (February 20, 1875): 25–26.

Supplément illustré. Figures contemporaines, 1893–1932.

Mariani's Coca Leaf. New York: Mariani & Co., 1902–06.

Books Published by Angelo Mariani

TALES ABOUT COCA AND VIN MARIANI

Arène, Paul. *Le Secret de Polichinelle.* Illustrated by A. Robida, Paris: H. Floury, 1897.

Arène, Paul, and Gustave Goetchy. *La fleur de Coca.* Pantomime, produced for the first and only time at the Théâtre Angelo Mariani, June 29, 1892. Paris: Impr. de Silvestre, 1892.

Beaumont, L. de. *Le Cas du Vidame.* Illustrated by A. Robida. Paris: Dentu, 1885; 2nd ed., Paris: Librairie illustrée, 1888.

———. *Sempervirens.* Illustrated by Ferdinand Lunel. Paris: H. Floury, 1896.

Bertheroy, Jean. *Cypsélos l'invincible.* Illustrated by Augustin Poupart. Paris: H. Floury, 1904.

Bouchor, Maurice. *Pervenche.* Illustrated by Léon Lebègue. Paris: H. Floury, 1900.

Christophle, Albert. *La rupture.* Illustrated by A. Robida. Paris: H. Floury, 1904.

Claretie, Jules. *Un chapitre inédit de Don Quichotte.* Illustrated by Atalaya. Paris: H. Floury, 1898.

———. *Explication.* Illustrated by A. Robida. Paris: Librairie illustrée, 1894.

Coutan, Germaine. *La Vengeance de la reine Zim, conte de fées.* Illustrated by the author. Paris, 1902.

Mistral, Frédéric. *Les Secrets des Bestes.* Illustrated by A. Robida,. Paris: H. Floury, 1896.

Bibliography of Published Works by and about Angelo Mariani

Montegut, Maurice. *Trois Filles et Trois Garçons.* Illustrated by Louis Morin. Paris: H. Floury, 1899.

Robida, Albert. *Le château de la grippe.* Illustrated by Émilie Robida. Paris: H. Floury, 1904.

Silvestre, Armand. *La Plante enchantée.* Illustrated by A. Robida. Paris: Librairie illustrée, 1895.

Uzanne, Octave. *La panacée du Capitaine Hauteroche.* Illustrated by Eugène Courboin. Paris: H. Floury, 1899.

OTHER TITLES

Arène, Paul. *Poésies.* Paris: A. Lemerre, 1900.

Brillat-Savarin, Jean Anthelme. *Les Aphorismes de Brillat-Savarin.* Paris: A. Blaizot, 1905.

Claretie, Jules. *Deux visions.* Illustrated by A. Robida. Paris: Angelo Mariani, 1910.

Mouchon, Louis Eugène. *Souvenirs, lettres à Angelo Mariani.* Frontispices, en-têtes et culs-de-lampe composés par l'auteur. Mesnil-sur-l'Estrée: Firmin-Didot, 1912.

Sand, George. *La Bonne Déesse de la pauvreté: Ballade.* Illustrated by Robida. Paris: Angelo Mariani, 1906.

Timoléon Pasqualini, Charles. *Choses du siècle et choses du cœur.* Paris: H. Floury, 1902.

Vossion, Louis. *Trois femmes pour un époux: Conte birman.* Illustrated by A. Robida. Paris: Angelo Mariani, 1910.

Documentary about Angelo Mariani

Delmon-Casanova, Jean-Luc. *Les Caprices de Mariani.* 2008, documentary, coproduced by Stella Productions and France 3, Corsica.

Main Works Dealing with Angelo Mariani

Note: Only books devoting at least two pages to Mariani are listed here. We have included page numbers where the information pertaining to Mariani can be found.

Alessandrini, Jean-Michel and Toussaint. *Le vin Mariani, ou l'histoire de la première boisson à la coca.* Biguglia, Corsica: Imp. Sammarcelli, 2001, 178 pages (among these, 152 pages are reproductions of Mariani's documents).

Andrews, George, and David Solomon, eds. *The Coca Leaf and Cocaine Papers.* New York: Harcourt Brace Jovanovich, 1975, 243–246.

Arren, Jules. *La publicité lucrative et raisonnée, son rôle dans les affaires.* Paris: Bibliothèque des Ouvrages Pratiques, 1909. 360–368 Reissued as *Sa majesté la publicité.* Tours: A. Mame et Fils, 1914, 167–174.

Ashley, Richard. *Cocaine: Its History, Uses and Effects.* New York: Warner Books, 1976, 55–59.

Avrane, Patrick. *Drogues et alcool: Un regard psychanalytique.* Paris: Campagne Première, 2007, 57–99.

Bachmann, Christian, and Anne Coppel. *Le Dragon domestique: Deux siècles de relations étranges entre l'Occident et la drogue.* Paris: Albin Michel, 1989, 102–105.

Basile, Jean. *Coca & cocaïne.* Montréal: Èditions de l'Aurore, 1977, 71–143.

Blaser, Franziska. "La poésie dans les *Albums Mariani*." Paper from the conference *Les Poètes et la publicité, Actes des Journées d'études des 15 et 16 janvier 2016,* 20–32, Université Sorbonne Nouvelle-Paris 3, 2017.

Bonaparte, Marie. *À la mémoire des disparus.* Vol. 2. *L'Appel des sèves.* Paris: P. U. F., 1958, 853–854.

Brun, Philippe. *Albert Robida (1848–1926): Sa vie, son œuvre.* Paris: Promodis, 1984, 52; 55.

Calvani, Sandro. *La coca: Passato e presente, Mito e realtà.* Cantalupa, Italy: Effatà, 2008, 60–62.

Delpirou, Alain. *Angelo Mariani, l'inventeur de la première boisson à la Coca.* Bastia, Corsica: Anima Corsa, 2014, 113 pages.

———. *Cocaïne. Histoire mondiale des drogues.* Bastia, Corsica: Anima Corsa, 2015, 86–91.

Delpirou, Alain, and Alain Labrousse. *Coca coke.* Paris: La Découverte, 1986, 31–40.

Domic, Zorka. *L'État cocaïne: Science et politique de la feuille à la poudre.* Paris: P. U. F., 1992, 69–75; 101–132.

Ducornet, Rikki. *Entering Fire.* San Francisco, CA: City Lights, 1987, 34–38; 81–82.

Durlacher, Julian. *Cocaïne.* Paris: Éditions du Lézard, 2000, 19–21.

Eyguesier, Pierre. *Comment Freud devint drogman.* Paris: Navarin Éditeur, 1983, 75–78; 95–116; 153–156.

Faux, Frédéric. *Coca! Une enquête dans les Andes.* Arles, France: Actes Sud, 2015, 39–41.

Gelsomini, Stefano. *Papa Leone XIII il vin Mariani e una strana pubblicità.* Carpineto Romano: n.p, 2013.

Ghozland, Freddy, and Henry Dabernat. *Pub & pilules: Histoires et communication du médicament.* Toulouse: Éditions Milan, 1988, 144–145.

Gootenberg, Paul. *Andean Cocaine: The Making of a Global Drug.* Chapel Hill: University of North Carolina Press, 2009, 25–29; 57; 61–62; 112; 115.

Grinspoon, Lester and James B. Bakalar. *Cocaine: A Drug and Its Social Evolution.* New York: Basic Books, 1976, 25–26; 30.

Hamowy, Ronald. *Dealing with Drugs: Consequences of Government Control.* Lexington, MA: Lexington Books. 1987, 189–190.

Helfand, William H.. *Quack, Quack, Quack: The Sellers of Nostrums in Prints, Posters, Ephemera and Books.* New York: The Grolier Club, 2002, 129–146.

Houche, Michel, and Stéphane Buttigieg. *Coca-Cola, la légende.* Sète, France: Flam Arts et Jardins, 2009, 12–16.

Julien, Jean-Rémy. *Musique et publicité: Du cri de Paris aux messages publicitaires radiophoniques et télévisés.* Paris: Flammarion, 1989, 147–156.

Julien, Pierre. "Angelo Mariani et son vin de coca: Mécénat et publicité," *Farmacia e industrializacion: Libro homenaje al doctor Guillermo Folch Jou.* Madrid: Sociedad Española de Historia de la Farmacia 1985, 115–135.

Bibliography of
Published Works by and
about Angelo Mariani

233

Karch, Steven B. *A Brief History of Cocaïne.* Boca Raton, FL: CRC Press, 1998, 23–29; 39; 101–102; 2nd ed. 2006, 31–42; 118.

Kennedy, Joseph. *Coca Exotica: The Illustrated Story of Cocaine.* Rutherford, NJ: Fairleigh Dickinson University Press and New York: Cornwall Books, 1985, 62–65; 83–87.

Lafont, René. *La Publicité pharmaceutique.* Paris: Librairie des Études de Vente, 1936, 250–261.

Lang, Jean-Pierre, and Guillaume Villemot. *Nés en Corse: L'extraordinaire aventure des inventions et des hommes qui ont changé la face du monde (et peut-être même celle de l'univers).* Ajaccio: Éditions des Immortelles, 2014, 10–19.

Lelong, Dr. *La coca du Pérou et ses applications thérapeutiques.* Paris: Clavel, 1883, 93–123.

Madge, Tim. *White Mischief: The Cultural History of Cocaine.* Edinburgh: Mainstream Publishing, 2001, 67–72.

Maillard, Léon. *Les Menus et programmes illustrés, invitations, billets de faire part, cartes d'adresse, petites estampes, du XVIIe siècle jusqu'à nos jours.* Paris: G. Boudet, 1898, 253–257.

Merkel, Howard. *An Anatomy of Addiction: Sigmund Freud, William Halsted, and the Miracle Drug Cocaine.* New York: Pantheon Books 2011, 54–58.

Mortimer, William G. *Peru: History of Coca, the "Divine Plant" of the Incas.* New York: J. H. Vail 1901, 177–181.

Neuilly-sur-Seine, Conseil general. *État des communes à la fin du XIXe siècle, publié sous les auspices du Conseil général. Neuilly-sur-Seine. Notice historique et renseignements administratifs.* Montévrain: Impr. de l'école d'Alembert, 1904, 180–181.

Nourrisson, Didier. *La saga Coca-Cola.* Paris: Larousse, 2008, 18–21.

Pendergrast, Mark. *For God, Country and Coca-Cola: The Unauthorized History of the Great American Soft Drink and the Company That Makes It.* New York: Collier Books, 1994, 24–26; 2nd ed. New York: Basic Books, 2000, 22–23.

Phillips, Joel, and Ronald D. Wynne. *Cocaine: The Mystique and the Reality.* New York: Avon Books, 1980, 50–52.

Rätsch, Christian, and Jonathan Ott. *Coca und kokain.* Aarau, Switzerland: AT Verlag, 2003, 84–87.

Reymond, William. *Coca-Cola: L'enquête interdite.* Paris: Flammarion, 2006, 56–61.

Richard, Denis. *La coca et la cocaïne.* Paris: P.U.F, 1994, 18–19.

Riotor, Léon. *Mariani l'Ange.* Annonay, France: Impr. de J. Royer, 1901, 26 pages.

Rivera Martinez, Edgardo. *Estampas de ocio, buen humor y reflexión.* Lima, Peru: UNMSM, Fondo Editorial, 2003, 69–73.

Romi. *Usines à gloire.* Paris: Éditions de Paris, 1956, 36–38.

Siegel, Ronald K. *Intoxication: Life in Pursuit of Artificial Paradise.* New York: Pocket Books, 1989, 266–269; 2nd ed., Rochester, VT: Park Street Press, 2005, 264–267.

Spillane, Joseph F. *Cocaine: From Medical Marvel to Modern Menace in the United States, 1884–1920.* Baltimore, MD: The John Hopkins University Press, 2000, 79–81; 129.

Stein, Pierre. *Tout savoir sur la cocaïne.* Lausanne: P. M. Favre, 1986, 73–90.

Streatfield, Dominic. *Cocaine.* London: Virgin Books, 2002, 61–63; 140.

Taillac, Pierre de. *Les paradis artificiels.* Paris: Hugo et Cie, 2007, 52–53.

Tracy, Jack, and Jim Berkey. *Subcutaneously, My Dear Watson: Sherlock Holmes and the Cocaine Habit.* Bloomington, IN: J. A. Rock, 1978, 38–41.

Walton, Stuart. *Out of It: A Cultural History of Intoxication.* London: Hamish Hamilton, 2001, 106–108.

Articles on Angelo Mariani

"Angelo Mariani." *Simple revue,* April 15, 1914, 225–27.

"Angelo Mariani et la presse." *Simple revue,* May 1, 1914, 258–61; May 15, 1914, 296–97; June 1, 1914, 323–24.

Armendares Pacreu, Carmina and Vicens Armendares Pacreu. "Angelo Mariani: Société, art, littérature et publicité III." (correspondence Mariani-Mistral), *La France latine,* no. 137 (2003): 13–139.

———. "Angelo Mariani II: Coca, cocaïne, publicité et littérature." *La France latine,* no. 130 (2000): 65–161;

———. "Autour de Mariani et son vin médicinal: documents." *La France latine,* no. 127 (1998): 91–147.

———. "Correspondance Mariani-Jeanne de Flandreysy." *La France latine,* no. 131 (2000): 163–204;

———. "Mariani et les bretons." *La France latine,* no. 133 (2001): 159–243, and no. 134 (2002): 185–255;

Beaumont, L. de. "Le vin Mariani." *Le Figaro,* July 13, 1896, 2.

Berr, Émile. "Un déjeuner de vernissage." *Le Figaro,* April 30, 1914, 1.

Betances. "L'album Mariani." *La fraternité,* no. 22 (1892): 2.

Bigeon, Armant. "L'affaire Reutlinger contre Mariani." *Bulletin du photo-club,* 1899, 1–9, 33–40.

Botes, Marietjie. "Vin Mariani—Saint or Sinner? Intellectual Property." *Without Prejudice,* no. 5 (June 2012): 33–34.

Claretie, Georges. "Figures contemporaine." *Le Figaro,* March 3, 1906, 1.

Cotinat, Louis. "Le Vin Mariani." *Le vieux papier,* no. 262 (October 1976): 537–39.

Davenay, G. "Le dixième tome de Mariani." *Le Figaro,* June 12, 1906, 2.

———. "Les obsèques de M. Mariani." *Le Figaro,* April 7, 1914, 3–4.

Delpirou, Alain. "Mariani et les cartes postales." *Le vieux papier,* no. 377 (July 2005): 314–18.

———. "Angelo Mariani, promoteur du vin à la coca." *Le Téléphonoscope* (Bulletin des amis d'Albert Robida), no. 19 (November 2012): 33–34.

Devaux, Guy. "Le Vin Mariani et sa publicité: Un intéressant recueil de Contes." *Revue d'histoire de la pharmacie,* no. 325 (2000): 131–32.

Doré, Sandrine. "Un artiste à la table d'Angelo Mariani, menus et publicités illustrés par Robida." *Le Téléphonoscope,* (Bulletin des amis d'Albert Robida), no. 14 (October 2007): 16–19.

Emery, Elisabeth. "Viral Marketing: Mariani Wine Testimonials in Early French and American Newspaper Advertising." *Nineteenth-Century Contexts* 39, no. 2 (May 2017): 117–29.

Evrard, Marie. "Au vin de coca Mariani." *Bulletin de la Société des amis d'Eugène Carrière,* March 9, 1998, 5–8.

Fernez, Pierre. "Mariani à Valescure . . . il y a 100 ans." *Courrier de Valescure,* no. 23 (March 1996): 6–9.

Gautier, Émile. "La coca considérée au point de vue scientifique et au point de vue industriel." *La science française,* June 24, 1898, 321–24.

———. "Le château Mariani." *Le Figaro,* December 1, 1904, 2.

———. "Figures contemporaines." *Le Figaro,* March 28, 1902, 3.

———. "Le triomphe du Vin Mariani." *Le Figaro,* October 27, 1903, 3.

Groff, John. "The Golden Age of Cocaine Wine: The Tonic of Popes and Presidents That Made the Gay Nineties Bubble." *High Times,* August–September 1975, 31–34.

Helfand, William H. "An Assay of Coca Wine: An Eyewitness Account." *Pharmacy in History* 30, no. 3 (1988): 155–56.

———. "Vin Mariani." *Pharmacy in History* 22, no. 1 (1980): 11–19.

Hill, David. "Art of Promotion: Mariani Medals at the ANS." *ANS Magazine,* no. 3 (2016): 40–51.

Julien, Pierre. "Les Contes à Mariani." *Revue d'histoire de la pharmacie,* no. 328 (2000): 522–24.

Lambert, Pierre. "Huysmans et le vin Mariani." *Bulletin de la société J. K. Huysmans,* no. 45 (1963): 53–54.

Langer, D. "La villa Andréa (villa Mariani)." *Simple revue,* May 1, 1910, 258–261.

Lara, René. "Angelo Mariani." *Le Figaro,* April 2, 1914, 3.

———. "Le miracle de la plante." *Le Figaro,* February 9, 1912, 1.

Leader. "Les champions du sport et le vin Mariani." *La vie au grand air,* suppl. 21 (May 1899): 2–3.

Lefebvre, Thierry. "Mariani versus Mariani." *Revue d'histoire de la pharmacie,* no. 332 (2001): 545–47.

La lettre de la Société des amis d'Angelo Mariani, Rennes, 2004–.

"Mariani contre hoirs Keisser." *Journal de jurisprudence commerciale et maritime,* 1888, 172–77; and *Journal des tribunaux de commerce,* 1888, 270–74.

Michaud-Jeannin, Emilie. "La nymphe de la Fontaine." *Var Matin,* September 2, 1990.

———. "Villa Andréa: Le souvenir d'Angelo Mariani." *Var Matin,* August 8, 1989.

———. "Villa Mariani, beauté architecturale anéantie." *Var Matin,* August 8, 1989, and November 6, 1990.

Nadal, Victor. "La coca et la cocaïne: Sommaire: leur rôle dans la thérapeutique; leur vulgarisation; les produits de M. Mariani." *Histoire du travail: Études littéraires sur les grandes industries, le commerce et l'agriculture,* 76, (1891).

Nede, André. "Envois de France." *Le Figaro,* March 10, 1913, 1.

———. "Fortuna . . .", *Le Figaro,* February 7, 1914, 1.

Ratoin, E. "La reproduction des photographies." *Le Monde artiste,* October 8, 1899, 652–653.

Raynal, Cécile. "Mariani versus Mariani: Jugement et rebondissement." *Revue d'histoire de la pharmacie,* no. 345 (2005): 100–101.

Régnal, Georges. "Angelo Mariani." *Nouvelle Revue,* May 15, 1914, 209–230.

Robida, Fred. "Mariani (1838–1914) mécène de la publicité." *Le vieux papier,* no. 260 (April 1976): 453–56.

Rouzet, Georges. "Léon Bloy, les frères Uzanne et le vin Mariani." *Bloyana,* no. 2, (September–October 1962): 6–9.

Smith, David. "Hail Mariani: The Transformation of Vin Mariani from Medicine to Food in American Culture, 1886–1910." *Social History of Alcohol and Drugs* 23, no. 1 (Autumn 2008): 42–57.

Trepardon, Francis. "Charles Gounod compose un hymne pour le Vin Mariani." *Revue d'histoire de la pharmacie,* no. 338 (2003): 313–15.

Uzanne, Joseph. "Figures de ce temps." *Le Figaro,* November 24, 1908, 3.

———. "Une innovation dans la publicité." *La publicité moderne,* no. 8 (August 1907): 8–11.

Uzanne, Octave. "Un don à la Bibliothèque Nationale." *Le Figaro,* November 25, 1909, 2–3.

Ververt. "Les Treize . . ." *Le Figaro,* January 20, 1911, 1.

"Vin Mariani: Official Report by Council on Pharmacy and Chemistry, with Comments Thereon." *Journal of the American Medical Association,* November 26, 1906, 1751–53.

Vital-Durand, Paul. "Suite aux 14 albums Mariani." *Le vieux papier,* no. 277 (July 1980): 80.

Vermeulen-Windsant, Charles, and Dean Latimer. "Vin Mariani: The Marvelous Elixir of Monsieur Mariani." *High Times,* April 1982, 64–68.

Viche, Jean-Claude. "Les Contes à Mariani écrits ou illustrés par Robida." *Le Téléphonoscope,* (Bulletin des amis d'Albert Robida), no. 19 (November 2012): 25–32.

Wrona, Adeline. "Des Panthéons à vendre: Le portrait d'hommes de lettres, entre réclame et biographie." *Romantisme,* no. 151 (2012): 48–50.

Index

Index